CLIMBING THE CORPORATE LADDER WITH SPEED

HOW TO BEGIN, MANAGE, CHANGE AND ACCELERATE YOUR CAREER TO EXECUTIVE MANAGEMENT

Dr. Fene Osakwe

BookSpider
EXPAND YOUR REACH

ISBN: 979-8-88759-305-0

Published by **BookSpider**

DOWNLOAD THIS FREE RESOURCE!

To say thank you for purchasing my book, I would like to give you this resource for free!
in larger font: 5 Questions to Know if You Are on the Right Career Path

SCAN ME

DOWNLOAD AT: feneo.authorchannel.co

TABLE OF CONTENTS

ACKNOWLEDGEMENTS

I owe the success of this book project to Almighty God, who gave me life and the wisdom to get my experiences and ideas distilled into this masterpiece that you now hold.

I am also grateful to my family for their unwavering support and understanding during the late nights of writing and crafting, especially to my loving wife, Damilola, who has been my greatest motivation in bringing this project to life. I cannot thank her enough for having my back always.

This book would not have come to life if I didn't have a story to share. To all the amazing people that I have worked with up to this point in my career – whether as colleagues, superiors, associates, or subordinates – I thank you for being a part of my story. My gratitude also extends to my wonderful friends who supported me in this journey

And to you, dear reader, who has seen value in this book and wants to learn something new about career success, I hope that what you are about to read beats your expectations and better equips you to move forward in your career regardless of what stage you are in at the moment.

PREFACE

Dear reader,

C*limbing the Corporate Ladder* is not just another book about how to excel and speed up your career. It is a book of hope and inspiration. Yes, you may not have had the best of backgrounds – you may not have attended the best of schools, had the opportunity to obtain an MBA or an international Master's degree, or have connections – yet you can climb to the very top of your career.

The road to success could be very tough, and people have different stories about their experiences. For some, it's about how they broke out of poverty through entertainment, sports, or business. For others, it's how they started their own business and got a fantastic investor who changed their story. However, there are not too many accounts of how people achieved the same by rising through the career ladder in the corporate world, and the reason for this is simple — careers confine you to a structure. That is, it is never about you but the organisation, so you are supposed to move at their pace.

For instance, in entertainment, you could get fortunate and be discovered by a promoter or producer while performing your craft. In football, an agent could sign you into a foreign club where you earn in USD/ Euros. In business, a single investor could change your fortunes overnight.

But careers do not work that way; they require that you begin from entry-level, acquire experience, and proceed gradually to the position of manager, senior manager, principal manager, associate director/director, and ultimately the senior or chief executive level.

This road is very long, it could sometimes take over thirty years.

If the task ahead fills you with self-doubt, with the feeling that you are not smart enough to get your career to where you envision it should be, know that you are not alone; I was once like you. I was never one of the best in class or any subject throughout my primary education and high school, and I never topped my class in any course in college. I didn't even know what it felt like to top a class throughout my schooling. I was the typical below-average student. The words 'flying colours' were alien to me.

Also, if you feel like you are not financially empowered enough to chase career success, I can relate to that. I have begged for money on the streets of Lagos because my transport fare was insufficient. I have had to sell books and other products on *Molue* in Lagos. A *Molue* is a modified Mercedes Benz of Bedford vehicle that carries between 90 to 120 passengers. My strategy was to leverage the large number of passengers in selling my products. I approached book vendors and product marketers and offered to help them sell off their goods inside *Molues.* The risk in this kind of business is that you could get robbed, and the profit margins are extremely small, you end up not making enough.

On other occasions, I have boarded buses praying the *conductors (*drivers' assistants who help coordinate bus fares, bus stops, and other bus operations*)* skip me by mistake as they collect the bus fare from passengers because I couldn't afford the fare. There were times my prayer got answered; other times, it didn't and left me with the options of either paying the bus conductor to drop me at the next bus stop or looking for a kind stranger who would allow me to sit on their lap throughout the bus ride.

Did I know people I could run to for handouts at this point in my life? Yes, I knew a few. But I was deliberate about taking control of my life instead.

The feeling of having already lost time could be most depressing sometimes. If this is your case, you have an understanding colleague in me. I failed so much in high school that I had to repeat it all over after graduating. I didn't pass any of the papers required to get into the higher institution. Guess what? I still didn't make those papers. Even though I finished my secondary school education (including the repeats) in the year 2000, I did not get into university until 2004

By implication, I was at home for four years (the average time required to complete a Bachelor's programme in Nigeria), unable to gain admission into the university, while my mates seemed to scale this hurdle effortlessly. It was not until many of them started graduating from the university that I was able to get in. That's not to mention that I also experienced my fair share of delays arising from the Academic Staff Union of Universities in Nigeria (ASUU) embarking on industrial action, such as strikes to press home their demands on the government

As I couldn't gain direct admission into the university, I had to go through a pre-degree programme. With a pre-degree programme, you have an alternative channel of getting in – if you're successful – and getting a degree.

However, suppose you do not succeed at your pre-degree; in that case, you only get a pre-taste of the university, and then you are sent back home – devastating!

Again if you feel that you have lost time, I can relate.

Perhaps, you are wondering how exactly you are supposed to get to the peak of your career – or even move up the ladder at all – having graduated from the university but without a good or satisfying job.

For me, after the long years in the university waiting to graduate, when I eventually started working, I was ashamed of associating with my peers because it seemed, at that time, that they all had better jobs than I did. So whenever we gathered, I shied away from conversations surrounding what we did or earned. I barely earned enough to cover my transportation then.

On one of the days I was working late, robbers attacked me with a gun pointed at my head. Everything I had – down to the belt which held my trousers around my waist — was stolen from me that day. I could barely afford airtime recharge or extra clothes. I started trying to get into comedy and music as entertainers seemed to have it going for them, but the prospects for me didn't seem promising.

So, if you have tried everything and it looks like all you need at this point is spiritual deliverance, know that my parents also thought the same of me once.

You see, in Africa where I'm from, when situations seem to defy logic or veer away from the expected course, our parents (and society) label your situation as 'spiritual' problems. They conclude that the person going through a tough time is demon-possessed, and this is not done out of hatred but rather limited knowledge and exposure.

How did I go from this phase of my life to becoming a technology executive in a multinational, Africa's most sought-after cybersecurity Advisor, and a Forbes Technology Council member within ten to eleven years? What did I do? What did I have to learn and unlearn? How did I compress time to make up for lost years? And who did I have to become to get to where I desired?

These are things I share with you in this book, and I hope that it connects with you in some way.

INTRODUCTION

If this appears to you like just another book on career acceleration, you may have to take a second look. You may already wonder what new thing you stand to gain from yet another book on career acceleration. Here, let me tell you. The contents of this book will change your perception of career development and growth in a way you never expected.

Acceleration here does not mean magic, a silver bullet, or getting overnight success tips. It is simply your capacity to gain speed in your career. There is an emphasis on your capacity because there is a place for personal responsibility.

One particularly inglorious trait that I have noticed among people who hail from what we have come to know as the 'third world' is our unconscious acculturation of giving excuses instead of taking responsibility for our actions and results in life. We easily believe, for instance, that the government or some external force or factor is to blame for every outcome we get, including where we are in our careers, the inadequate infrastructure in our countries, the ailing educational system, and so on.

While it is true that some of these challenges are prevalent in our society and constitute bottlenecks in many ways, it would be largely erroneous to see them in light of the major barriers to your progress in life and career. Perhaps these excuses are sometimes tenable, yet accepting them as insurmountable hurdles on your path to success in any endeavour will probably keep you in the same spot for years.

This self-limiting stereotypic thought pattern of scarcity and insurmountable challenges appears to be the prevalent influence on people's interpretation of life these days.

What do I mean? For instance, if a person served in the government for thirty-five years and finally got into senior-level management before retiring, such a person would be highly applauded in society, especially in Africa. This naturally breeds the assumption that it takes thirty-five years to reach the peak of a career in such a field. But could this feat be achieved a lot earlier than that? We usually do not pay attention to the possibility of such. This is how we became wired to believe that success takes protracted time to manifest.

Another effect of this is that we have unconsciously rested our beliefs on the falsehood that people who succeed early in life either did so through fraudulent means or are well connected to someone on the top who helped them or that they paid someone somewhere to get where they are. This mindset calcifies the belief that success in life and career is too herculean to be possible, and those who achieved it within a shorter time, outside of the norm, must have cut corners in some way.

There is also the unfounded assumption that a good role model is hard to find since many of the successful men and women celebrated in society today cannot categorically tell you 'how' they got to where they are, as some stumbled on it by chance and some others did certain things that cannot be known or explained to the public.

And so, we continue to celebrate and replicate stories of this kind while accepting an average life. We think success must require some unholy assistance and exchange – which is entirely false.

This is the narrative I seek to change through this book. For a fact, I was able to get to a top-level position at a multinational company in ten years just by strictly adhering to some powerful values and principles without any form of corner-cutting or godfather- clinching.

Therefore, I have carefully documented my career success journey and the principles I applied in this book.

As you read, your mindset towards success, particularly career success, will change as you are inspired by my story and instructed by the principles I followed. In addition, I will also give you practical steps on how to do exactly what I did to achieve better results.

However, this would require that you embrace a growth mindset, be willing to learn new things, and unlearn some old, unproductive, and limited knowledge, bearing in mind that you can be a source of inspiration to many after you – you are already a life and career role model to someone you may not even know.

This book will show you how to take personal responsibility for your life and career by intentionally taking steps toward your goals. You will also learn:

- How to set goals in line with your objectives and create actions to follow through
- Steps to take to become an Industry leader in your field
- How to play office politics
- How to develop and leverage relationship capital in the office
- How to plan for your retirement in your thirties

It also opens your minds to possibilities that:

- It is possible to be a CEO, CSO, or Director in a multinational company worth billions of dollars in your thirties without cutting corners.
- It is also possible to have good role models who have done the things you seek to achieve and can hold you by the hand on the steps they took.
- You can reach the peak of your career in your early forties without having to work for forty-two or forty-five years.

As you read this book, I am going to show you:

- How
- What to do
- What not to do
- When to do
- And most importantly, the things I did to achieve accelerated career success.

The preface already captured a brief about my journey – from where I started to where I am privileged to be today. I believe you can replicate the same, and even better, in a shorter time frame.

I sincerely hope that you enjoy this book and find the needed knowledge to apply as you give your career the boost it needs.

Cheers.

PART I

STARTING OUT IN YOUR CAREER

How do you start your career? Why choose a particular career path? How do you weigh your options and decisions with regard to your talents, passion, training, or academic experience?

These are some of the many questions that remain unanswered in the minds of many aspiring and established career people today. Choosing a career is always a big struggle for most people because it is a critical juncture where they need to make one of life's defining decisions.

Sometimes, this indecisiveness sets in when people are interested in more than one career path or are unsure how they will perform if they decide to stick to a particular field. Other times, people are just obsessed with wanting to be at the top of their game or making as much money as possible, they are willing to take any career path.

It is common to see people choose a career path because it is popular. After all, 'if everyone is doing it, then it has to be yielding something good', you will often hear many of them say.

Yet the questions every career-conscious person must ask are: Do I want the most popular field or the one most fulfilling for me and impactful to society for years to come? Is this field worth getting into just because of the prestige it commands, or do I have the passion that aligns with it? Lastly, when I step into this career path, are my foundations strong enough to preserve me till I retire?

And Then, there is the question: How do I retrace my steps if I think I have got it all wrong? Have I set reasonable goals and plans? How long am I willing to wait until I see results?

These are core questions you will find answers to as you read through the chapters in this part.

CHAPTER 1

THE FIRST FEW STEPS

One of the many interesting parts of watching a baby grow is looking out for when and how they take their first few steps in life. Such moments are usually defining and memorable for parents who would already have brimming expectations of seeing their baby get up from the ground, stand on their feet, and move the first foot in the right direction.

This is quite similar to how people start out in their careers. Just as babies are largely unconcerned about how or what their first steps look like, career newbies are usually not intentional about taking the first few steps in their careers. Some others do not at all take the start of their career seriously. This lack of preparation and intentionality is the reason many people encounter challenges later.

But, like a baby learning to master the first few steps in life would sometimes need a hand to hold for stability, consider this chapter a trusted hand to help you take your first steps in your career or retrace your steps if you have gone some distance and felt something is missing.

Goals

If you asked me what the first step to climbing the corporate ladder is, I would easily tell you that it is goal-setting. Goal setting is one important step that helps you to know where you are going, what you want to achieve, and how you want to achieve it. It is fundamental to building your career and in other areas of life.

Nothing takes form or shape in this world without first being envisioned, pre-defined, planned, and actively worked on. Research has also shown that the top 1% in every organisation have their goal clearly written out.

Without a goal, the various parts of an organisation would lack coordination in their activities. This could be detrimental if the activities carried out are contrary to the advancement of the organisation's plans and growth. If goals are not set, there will be no road map or blueprint to achievable heights and success in anything.

For instance, one thing that makes football matches interesting is goals. If goals don't exist, then the whole activity would be meaningless. It would only be a crowd of men and women running back and forth without direction.

Unfortunately, this is how many people run their lives, especially their careers. If you ask an average person about his career goals, you'll hear him mention unrealistic things he never planned to work toward. Some just want to hit the jackpot or get lucky somehow. But life doesn't work that way.

And to be clear, 'jackpot' in this context is not a lottery. If you want to become a banker just because you saw someone driving a G-wagon on your street, or you want to go into tech just so you can afford what you see others possess, that is a jackpot mentality. There is a clear difference between being inspired and building castles in the air. If you want to relocate to a different country just because you saw someone who relocated there become more successful, you have this same mentality.

You need to be clear on the difference between what a goal is and the means to achieving that goal.

Without a clear plan or objective, you can never achieve your goals. If you are not clear on where you want to be

– for instance, in ten years – it will be hard to achieve your plans.

What Qualifies as a Goal?

A goal is an idea of the result you desire through planning and commitment. Creating goals without corresponding plans is tantamount to creating a wish list. There must be laid down practical steps to take to achieve those goals. Genies grant wishes, but career achievements are a response to proper planning. For example, wishing to be a director of a multi-billion-dollar company is fantastic – anyone could wish for that. Creating clear-cut plans and commitment to that objective is what distinguishes wishes from goals.

People admire those at the top and wish to be like them, but the plans to achieve that are left to chance because there are a lot of assumptions that things happen automatically and what will be will be. This is a wrong mindset that we must intentionally eliminate.

One of my goals as a student was to work in a multinational company. Therefore, I sought the requirements for working where I wanted to be and worked towards it.

Any career goal you cannot begin to do something about now becomes a wish list. So, you must break your goals down into plans that are achievable within a certain amount of time.

Do You Have the Right Motive?

One of the most critical drivers to setting your goals is your motives.

People gravitate towards particular career paths for different reasons, and this influences the goals they pursue on such career paths. Sometimes, it could be that they want to impress someone, prove to people that they have arrived, or just be named among people on that career path.

Remember that at some point in your journey, life will ask you, 'why?' It is important to get this right because when challenging times come, your why will sustain you. If it is fuelled by wrong motives, you will be frustrated and probably give up or seek shortcuts.

Throughout my journey, one of the reasons I had the discipline to stick to my plans in line with achieving goals was my 'why'. It drove why I could not cut corners, offers I could take or not take, and some discomfort I had to persevere.

Another point to note is that depending on your objectives, the demands that would be made of you will differ from someone else's. For instance, the demands for a person who wants to run a 400-metre race in 10 minutes are different for another person who wants to run the same race in 4 hours.

Some do not care how long it takes them to achieve their goals as long as they are comfortable where they are. But a genuine goal always has a time limit.

Setting Clear Career Goals

Setting career goals is tied to the 'where', 'why', and 'when' of those goals. 'Where do I want to be?', 'Why do I want to be there?' and 'When do I want to be there?'

Yes, there's a general belief that you must follow your passion when setting goals – like it's the first thing to do – but I believe doing that may not necessarily hold true for pursuing career growth. Not every passion can be backed by relevant long-term goals; you might end up frustrated when you have no substantial result to show.

Sticking to your passion should not be an obstacle to exploring other opportunities.

There is a general belief that you must narrow your life down to your passion and nothing else. However, when you explore other fields that you possibly have the potential to handle, you will be surprised at how much growth and success you derive from them.

When setting career goals, there is need to seek advice from a mentor. It is not wise to create career goals in the isolation of a mentor. As previously stated, to achieve a goal, you need to meet people who have achieved that goal before you – exactly what I did.

Career goals are created in context. For instance, you need to know what kind of career will be relevant in the next ten years.

When I started in cyber security, I realised that people did not consider it a big deal. So, I sought those who were authorities in that field and reached out to them. I was enlightened that people who had begun to create data and information into soft copies will eventually seek how to protect them, just as they seek security for their physical properties. Therefore, it was important for people to begin gaining knowledge in this field. Though only a few did at that time.

Through proper guidance, I was able to know that this was the field I could go into that would be relevant for many years. But, mind you, my passion was entirely different.

Another thing to note when setting career goals is the success rate. You cannot set career goals in an area where the probability of success is extremely low. Know the areas you are interested in, and then seek someone to guide you in choosing the right career.

In my case, when I started out in IT, I had to choose either hardware or software, so I checked out the average payment of the professionals I saw in both hardware and software; this made my decision easy because, at that time, I realised that software was more profitable financially. You can also apply this strategy to other fields, be it sports, entertainment, trading, or consulting.

Furthermore, use the success rate around you, not the success stories you read in the media that are hyped. You should know that those stories often stand out and get a lot of 'hype' because those stories are exceptions to the rule.

Values to Hold Dear

The core values I held on to uncompromisingly are:

1. Having career goals and writing them out
2. Defining my why.
3. Staying committed and disciplined
4. Having daily plans, tasks, and milestones in line with my goals
5. Give it what it takes, not your best, as your best may not be enough

A person's values directly show the relationship between them and their goals. Values are motivating or guiding beliefs that steer or encourage attitudes and behaviours. They are unique to individuals and fundamental to the actions one takes and how individuals react and interpret situations in life. Your values determine if you will either go all the way to achieve your goals, give up halfway, seek a powerful person to make your journey easier, or bribe your way through.

Your values do not let you settle for whatever comes. Rather, they push you to strategise, reconstruct, and determine your outcomes in your career. There are principles to everything in life. If you can use your mind's imaginative power to envision your career, then you can set proper goals to actualise them.

A man without a vision is a man without a purpose. A vision is a future caused by dedicating ourselves and committing our resources to fulfil our goals, while a purpose is a determination we have towards that vision.

In the next chapter, I will begin to give practical examples that will stir you up to take the right steps early.

CHAPTER 2

CHOOSING THE RIGHT CAREER PATH

Life is like a cocoon that contains the elements of time; your career will mostly require a huge portion of your apportioned time. Therefore, the journey to figuring out and eventually choosing the right career for yourself is an important part of your life that you need to pay attention to and be intentional about.

In this part of the world – precisely Africa – we grew up inculcating the belief that the best careers are strictly in Medicine, Law, Engineering, Accounting, Economics, or other courses of similar colouration; careers outside the known mainstream are stamped as 'child's play'. Those career paths were what worked for the old generation; hence this mindset has flowed down many generations. They saw several successful doctors, lawyers, engineers, etc. So, pushing their kids to fit into those career paths felt justifiable.

For example, my parents wanted me to be a medical doctor, which wasn't a wrong career path, but it was not right for my journey.

We may find ourselves doing the same with our children as we place them into the entertainment industry, social media, or tech because there are many successful people in it. Though it sounds less restrictive than what our parents wanted, it's fundamentally still the same principle. We see what has worked and try to get our kids on the same path. It's important to guide but not to exact force.

Why Go Where?

What makes a particular career path right for you? I believe no career is wrong, only that people step into what isn't right for them. This means that the career path is not the problem, but being right for you is the fit you must find.

The real estate and the finance and investment sectors, for example, are said to have produced the highest number of millionaires. Nevertheless, they have also produced people who lost millions. So, getting it right is key.

Here are some things to consider before stepping into a career path. Note that this list is not in any way exhaustive.

- **Values**

Values are fundamental standards, beliefs, or principles you hold dear. They guide your attitude, behaviour, perspectives, and interpretations in life. For instance, if your value system does not condone taking another person's life, then starting a career in the military or police force may not be for you. You might find yourself in situations where you have to take actions that could conflict with your values.

Therefore, your career must not conflict with your values but align with them. You should also know that prioritising your core values can help you discover your niche and foster your fulfilment in your chosen career.

- **Financial Goals**

Your financial goals are also contributing factors to figuring out your career path. For instance, they could be based on the following:

What are your short, long, and mid-term goals? When do you want to become a millionaire? When do you want to own a property, get married, etc.? Certain disciplines can make this happen in about forty years, while others make these goals achievable in a shorter time frame.

If you choose a career that pays you less than you anticipated without the potential to pay you enough to achieve your goals, your performance and productivity will wane.

- **High-Income Skills**

With the way technology is shaping the world, certain skills now have high demand. These are referred to as high-income skills because of the timeline for acquiring them and the number of jobs available on those paths. For example, a skill in robotics would pay you higher than a skill in fashion designing, not necessarily because robotics is better than fashion designing, but because of the demand and how much resources a person requires to acquire a skill in robotics.

Therefore, it is important that you do extensive research and ensure that you equip yourself with high-income skills. People earn way over a hundred thousand dollars just because they have these skills.

- **Academic Background**

While your course in school may not ultimately decide where or what career path you choose, it can give you leverage. For example, it is difficult to apply for a nursing role when you study engineering, or apply for tech roles as a graduate of international relations. Of course, you can get trained for the new career you desire, but the point is your academic background should not be totally discarded.

- **Passion**

Some motivational speakers tell you to follow your passion, although your passion might not be the right career path for you. You will ultimately need to be passionate about what you do. But if you follow your passion without knowledge, understanding, and counsel, then, in the long run, your passion could become an extinct skill or difficult to monetise.

I once had a mentee who was extremely passionate about typing. He could type a whole book in a few hours, and he began to train people on it. But now, software has been developed to do what he does, so regardless of how passionate he is about typing, he is no longer needed for it. For someone like me who loves driving, I didn't interpret that passion as a lead to a career path; instead, I could probably leverage technology to convey people to places, e.g., Uber.

The new opportunities in this digital age require open-mindedness, curiosity, and a willingness to learn. Just make sure to explore opportunities and give room for growth.

- **Seek for Exposure**

Seek to be exposed to various professions in order to weigh your options and know exactly where you want to go. I will use a food illustration here: You may think that rice with chicken is your best food if that's all you've been exposed to for years. But the day you have an intercontinental buffet, your mind will begin to open up to other possibilities, and you'll start to think differently about your best food.

Truly, it is difficult to desire what you haven't been exposed to. Therefore, find out from people in various professions about what they do and how they do it. That way, your mind begins to see other opportunities.

- **Demand and Supply in Fields**

It's advisable to examine the supply and demand patterns in various career paths. Is there a great demand in the market for that career you admire?

I noticed that in my field, the demands constantly exceeded the supply, while in some other fields, it is the other way round. I knew people working in banks, the media industry, and law firms who stated they had experts in IT. This confirmed the advice I got from my career guides 'With IT, you can work anywhere'. I immediately knew that IT was where I was going.

Research shows that there will be 3.5 million cybersecurity job posts in three years without skilled people to fill them globally. So, what is the prediction in your field or the field you want to go into? This leads me to my next point.

- **Conduct Adequate Research**

Unlimited access to a plethora of information on the internet gives you insight into the career path you are interested in. However, due to the subjective nature of people who place information in public for commercial purposes, it is more valuable to get first-hand information or tips from people who have achieved certain heights in their careers. They could be in the same field you want to step or elsewhere.

Additionally, do research on future careers that are yet to be developed. Through this, you will know what experts say about jobs that will go extinct and the ones you could consider preparing for.

Dealing With Career Progression Myths

If you've ever discussed a career path with people, chances are that you have been given some advice based on subjective opinions and ideas. Even your parents have opinions and desires on the right career path for you. People have myths about everything in life, including career paths.

Myths are misconceptions and concocted explanations for events and phenomena. They are commonly held but might be false. People have unprovable conclusions and judgments about certain career paths; how to go about having a successful career, how long it would take, and what is possible and impossible to achieve. These myths should have no place when you set out to map out a career path. I believe the best way to refute myths is to find people who have successfully changed the narrative based on their results.

Some of the career myths I heard about for some years, and found to be false, are mentioned below:

- **Myth 1 – You must perfectly match job requirements**

This is mostly for entry-level roles. We are in a dispensation where soft skills such as communication, emotional intelligence, teamwork, problem-solving, and a can-do attitude are as relevant to many organisations as technical skills. You do not necessarily need to have many years of experience to become an asset. I didn't, either. In fact, after my youth service (a one-year service that Nigerians render to the nation after graduating from tertiary institutions), my first job was in a finance role, which was not on par with my first degree in Computer Science.

If you are willing to get groomed and learn new things quickly, you can start from there. The reason for this shift is that certificates do not always equate to individuals' abilities, effectiveness, and productivity. Most skills are learnable over a period of time, if you are willing.

Although, as you grow in your career and get more specialised, it becomes highly unlikely that you aren't the perfect match for jobs in your field. However, at the entry-level, more emphasis is placed on soft skills, attitude, and a readiness to learn.

- **Myth 2 – Strictly follow your passion**

Your passion may not be something you would love to do as a full- time job for an extended period.

The dictionary definition of passion speaks to strong or barely controllable emotions. However, one of the things I've learnt experientially about emotions is that they change. So, it's not something you can completely rely on; it is not wise to build one hundred per cent of your career, goals, and aspirations simply on emotions.

Although you must indeed be passionate about what you plan to do or what your hands find to do, still, your passion needs guidance, research, and mentorship.

The point is that it is risky to create a career path based solely on your passion – you may wind up quitting earlier than you anticipated.

- **Myth 3 – You don't have any leadership skills**

Leadership is borne out of a substantial experience in leading and guiding a team of people to attain a goal. You don't necessarily need to have had leadership experience in the field you want to go into; you could have it somewhere else because it's mainly the same class of challenges all leaders face, irrespective of their field.

For instance, during my first job interview for a finance function, I was asked if I had leadership experience. Obviously, I didn't have one in the area of the job I was being interviewed for, as I was still fresh out of school. So I told my interviewer about my leadership experience in church. He asked how and what I did, and I explained how I coordinated specific projects to achieve church objectives with my team and the results we achieved, including the feedback we got.

You shouldn't beat yourself up because your experience is not in the area of the job you want.

Furthermore, leadership skills need to be consistently nurtured as you grow. Therefore, you must expose yourself to training and books. Also, as you upgrade your leadership skills, you need to know the technicalities of being a successful leader, such as organisation, stability, quick decision-making, problem-solving, conflict resolution, effective communication, active listening, and more. These virtues are not entirely results of genetics but can be acquired.

- **Myth 4 – It takes several years to get promoted to an executive/management position**

I can't stress enough how much this is untrue. You do not have to spend thirty or forty years to reach the peak of your career; you can get to great heights if you constantly develop yourself and progressively deliver at your job. I did it in nine years; you can do it in less. I spent six years moving from entry-level to manager level, eight months from being a manager to becoming a senior manager, one and a half years from a senior manager to an associate director, and six months to becoming a director.

I have a friend who once went for an entry-level orientation at a bank, and during the process, an executive director came to speak to the new candidates. He stated that only one per cent of them would make it to his current level because he had spent 38 years in the field to get to that point. Imagine how demoralising that must have been for entry-level candidates.

The point is that getting to the top is tied to the value you can provide at that level, not the years you have spent. Most times, the expectation is that the more years spent, the more understanding of the business you will have, and you will also be able to provide good value.

- **Myth 5 – What will be, will be**

Ending up as a successful career person requires proper strategies and goals, with all intentionality and investment of time and other resources. It's a journey with an objective; a means to an end.

Many leave their career paths to chance and just go to work every day, waiting for their organisation to declare promotions and promote them. If they get promoted, they are ok ; if they don't get promoted, they are fine. Whether they move or not, they are not concerned. This is what we call in Nigeria the 'I cannot kill myself' mentality. And this simply means you are not willing to take responsibility for your growth. You have practically outsourced it to your organisation to determine when you can or cannot move.

Therefore, you have to be intentional and take responsibility for your career growth if you want to attain a certain height.

Career myths can stop you from seeing your many possibilities and options. Therefore, you should not accept career stereotypes because they can limit you from exploring other career paths, discovering the unknown capacity in you, and growing strategically.

One thing you cannot do is stop people from having their perspectives and impressions about certain career paths. However, if your career path is among some of those often stereotyped, then be intentional about changing the narrative through professionalism and excellence. Artistry, for instance, has been overlooked and narrowed down to paintings for the purpose of entertainment; meanwhile, it has so many dimensions and expressions that very few explore.

Finally, seek career guidance from more experienced people who can provide informed, objective, and reliable answers to your questions.

CHAPTER 3

LANDING YOUR FIRST JOB

For many career professionals, one of the most unforgettable moments in their career story is when they got their first job and the events leading up to that employment. It is usually a moment to remember for many because of the uncertainty and self-doubt that comes with their inexperience. At this stage, even something as regular as crafting CVs, preparing for interviews, answering interview questions with confidence, etc., can appear daunting for career newbies.

At this stage, many are unsure why they are not being called for job interviews, doubt that their CV is well written, and get lost on the internet searching for the right CV template among the innumerable ones available.

Their uncertainty lingers even at the interview stage. Until an interview lands them a job – their first job – they usually are in doubt about their performance. They will often wonder what action or inaction, special oomph lacking in their qualifications, could deprive them of their dream job.

Does this sound like you, dear reader? Well, don't be disturbed. We've all been there too.

Typically, you would think this anxiety should end after getting your first job, but no, it goes beyond getting an offer letter. It feels as though you are suddenly plunged into a sea of people who appear to have it all figured out. You likely have not had the opportunity to work in such a structured place that demands taking on corporate responsibilities and maintaining formal relationships. You are not sure who to ask for or what counts as unprofessional.

This chapter takes you through the practical steps for maximising all the opportunities around you to land your first job and what you should do to start well. With this, your attempts will be strategic and targeted, and you will be assured of your efforts without feeling like you are taking a shot in the dark.

Identifying and Latching On to Job Opportunities

In addressing the search for job opportunities, I would like to start by talking about perseverance. I have found out that one of the problems with our generation is that we are quick to give up. This attitude is fuelled by the mentality that there are few options, so we simply look around for anything that works.

I have mentored many people who, on the verge of giving up, would say, 'I have been applying to this company for the past six months', 'I have sent out job applications to so many companies with no response, I am tired'.

The first thing I do is tell my story – how I sent out over 250 applications and even started applying to job posts requesting money to help you with a job. Even though I knew it reeked of a scam, I was just too desperate to get a job.

The truth is that sometimes, what you need to get that first job may be a tweak in your CV, leverage a relationship, or simply wait for your time. You may need to re-strategise, polish your skills, improve your knowledge, and try again.

One of my mentees got a job with an international company headquartered in the United States of America. But before then, he had been job-hunting for four and a half years! Sharing my job-hunting story with him and taking him under my mentorship encouraged him. It also motivated him to apply some of the principles I shared earlier, the rest of which I will share as this book progresses.

Imagine how difficult it must have been for him to survive without a job for over four years before eventually landing an exceptional job at a multinational company. But today, all those experiences are behind him. His two-month salary wiped away the pain of four years, and he flies around the world now.

Anyone searching for a good job should be willing to persevere because not everybody gets called after their first application.

It also bears mentioning that in the absence of a society where a good job awaits every qualified person, we must recalibrate our mindsets to get the best out of the current state of affairs. This, for example, means that we may need to shift from the mindless **search for jobs** to the **search for job opportunities**.

Though they might appear to be the same, they are not quite so. Many people remain without worthwhile employment for protracted periods due to the inability to recognise job opportunities. When what they want does not come in the package that they desire, they overlook it.

While the dream may be to work in a large company with mouth- watering remuneration, the greater priority for an entry-level professional should be finding a place to hone their competencies.

Admittedly, some people find these two packages in one place, but it doesn't work that way all the time. To get to your desired career, you may need to take up smaller but related jobs that give you the skills and experience you need to thrive in the bigger place.

I remember having to stay and work in the same company where I did my NYSC just to continue gaining experience. It was an IT start- up company with five staff at the time.

The NYSC (National Youth Service Corps) in my country Nigeria is a federal government scheme that mandates all university graduates to serve the country for one year. The graduates working under the NYSC scheme are deployed to other regions of the country and paid a stipend by the government every month. The ultimate aim of the scheme is to encourage inclusion and diversity, especially among the youth. However, because of how the NYSC is run, jobs taken up by the corps members during the service year are not considered full-scale jobs, so they typically have to begin the hunt for proper jobs at the end of the programme.

That was in 2010, and I was paid N15,000 (about $90 at the time) as a monthly salary. Yet, many of my entry-level contemporaries who worked at banks and multinationals received N120,000 salary, about $626. You would agree with me that that was a huge salary margin.

Sometimes you don't have what you want in your career at a point in time, but your diligence, willingness to learn, and ability to focus on the goal are what will help you extract the best value from that opportunity. Mine was a small company, but I made it a learning ground.

To be clear, I am not implying that you should abandon your aspirations. I did not do so either. I wanted to practice IT at the highest level, and this was a small IT company that wasn't paying well but a place where I could hone my skills in line with my career objectives. So, as I worked at that first job of mine, I actively sought other ones.

One time, a multinational company that had just set up business in Lagos was recruiting, and I was caught in a stampede that occurred. That was in early 2010. The company had invited graduates with first-class and upper second-class honours for a test, and I was shocked to meet a mammoth crowd at the venue despite the filtering by qualification. It was chaotic that day; about twenty people fainted. The news made it to major Nigerian newspapers.

On another occasion, I fell into the wrong hands. In Nigeria, at that time, oil and gas was the foremost lucrative industry; they were a big deal. I had seen an oil and gas job advert and decided to go for the opportunity. I, as well as other interested applicants, paid some money and then headed to the University of Lagos, the supposed venue of the entry-level oil and gas recruitment exam. We realised we had been swindled only after arriving there and meeting no one. But despite these misadventures, I refused to give up on my aspirations.

I eventually lost that first entry-level job of mine at some point, but because many of the company's clients knew me and missed our relationship, they sought after me to handle some of their IT projects. Suddenly, I began to earn way more from these gigs than I'd ever earned as a full-time employee. I even went on to buy my first car from the earnings during this freelancing period.

Yes, this might be an inspiring story, but do remember that I developed and honed all the skills that helped me survive amid my unemployment in my last job, the same one that had paid me 'peanuts'.

So, start small, as long as it aligns with your goal. Don't give up; keep pushing.

Handling Job Interviews

Later, I will share tips on how to ace mid and senior-management interviews. This section, however, is dedicated to entry-level interviews. I will use practical examples from my experiences to highlight things to look out for, what to do, and what to avoid.

About eleven years ago, I got called for an interview by one of the big four global professional service firms after writing and passing their recruitment test. But before I share some of the questions I was asked, I must mention that there is no one-size-fits-all trick to passing interviews. Interviews occur at different levels, so what is considered admissible in an entry-level, one-year, or two-year experience-level interview may not be permissible as you ascend the career ladder.

For example, an interview question like – 'Have you led a team before?' At the entry-level, it is okay to say no, but at the senior management level, it may not be acceptable. This is because, at this level, it is expected that you are able to coordinate people in achieving your objectives.

Some of the questions they asked during my first interview include:

- **'What value are you bringing to the organisation?'**

I found this question amusing, and that's because I expected that my interviewers would understand I had a few months of experience outside my NYSC. What was I supposed to be bringing to the table? And this is where I think many job applicants miss it too.

When asked the question above, do not try to impress with your answer. As a newbie in your profession, there isn't much you are bringing to the table aside from your basic experience and willingness to improve yourself while executing the new role. Your recruiters know this. Therefore, always bear in mind that what they want to deduce from your response is your hunger and desire to learn as well as your willingness to apply yourself and your skills to the tasks at hand.

In answering the question, I explained how I was a fast learner and would learn quickly and bring innovation to how things were done, as I did in my final year project in school – which was really the only project I had done at the time.

- **'What is your five-year plan?'**

I answered this question within the context of the company. Many job applicants commit the blunder of talking about a grand plan that does not involve the company. What this communicates to the person interviewing you is: 'I don't see a future with your company', 'I do not exactly buy into your vision; I am only here in the interim'.

Although the desire to start one's career in a company and then progress to other dream jobs is legitimate, it is equally important to show selflessness in relating with your potential employers. No one wants to hire a parasite whose only desire is to take without giving back, so you must learn to be tactful when responding to such.

- **'What is your salary expectation?'**

By all means, be bold in your request, but do not be absurd. Absurdity is when your request far outweighs the industry's or company's standard pay. When you ask for remuneration that is way above your experience, it betrays a lack of adequate research on your part, and you won't be taken seriously. Your request will only be regarded as a random wish.

As an entry-level applicant, your safest course of action will be to acknowledge that the company has a salary structure for the role and to request to know what this structure is. Then, ask them their budget for your role, and you can negotiate your pay (As you grow, you can demand more).

That's what I did years ago, and it worked. I know it did because I passed the Big Four consulting firm's interview and got my employment letter. And not only that, but I also received feedback from them that my interview answers were impressive because I gave the right type of answers.

This response is fine for entry-level. However, for an experienced hire, the response will be different. Most times, the increase you are asking for should be a percentage of what you currently earn. And although there are different opinions about this approach from human resource practitioners, it is still the norm. Some persons will ask for a 50% or 70% increase, while others will ask for a 500% or 700% increase.

I have sat in interviews where people make such requests, and the panel sees them as greedy or not having any sense of understanding about what is expected at their level. But if you are required to relocate to another country that probably uses a different currency, then you may even ask for a higher percentage increase.

I will now go on to mention a few more interview experiences, which, although they are not mine, I believe you can learn from. They are areas where I have seen people stumble, and I hope that you don't.

- **'Tell us a bit about yourself'.**

This is one question every job applicant must prepare for. When this occasion arises, it is time for you to sell yourself by pointing out key experiences and how they are relevant to the role and potentially add value to the company. Also, be careful not to sound overconfident.

This has to be said, as millions of printed and digital content constantly talk about the importance of confidence during an interview. And while this is a good thing, many people either abuse or misinterpret the message. So, yes, it is important to show up for your interview self-assured and with calm nerves, but this should not be an invitation to get too casual with the opportunity.

I remember a young man I interviewed a few years ago as assistant manager. When I asked that he briefly tell the panel about himself, he replied, 'Can I just bring out my CV and read my profile?' Perhaps, he felt our asking him that question was redundant since the information we wanted was contained in his CV.

Another applicant I interviewed was a hardware engineer with about two years of experience. One could tell he knew his craft and was quite confident of his chances, but he overplayed his hand by getting too casual during his interview. He would drag out his speech when answering his questions, repeatedly cross and uncross his legs, and roll around in his swivel chair. He went as far as correcting questions we posed to him.

Unfortunately for him, all the panel had to do was ask him a few questions out of his comfort zone and his countenance turned almost pitiable. He lost his chance, of course.

Jumping at every opportunity to correct interviewers is the wrong approach to impressing them or asserting your competence. Not only does it depict arrogance and a lack of tact, but it also betrays a tendency to display insubordination if employed. You should, therefore, mind your words and tone while not forgetting to pay attention to your gestures and general carriage.

Dealing With Rejections

You prepared earnestly for the interview. You gave the written and oral tests your best shot. But regardless of how well you think you may have performed, there's always the element of unpredictability that follows interviews.

Perhaps you did well, but what if you were not the only one who performed excellently? Or did you even perform excellently at all? You stalk your email almost every hour of the day, expectant. And finally, you receive the message, but it comes with the dreaded word, 'Unfortunately...'

Rejection can be devastating. For many job applicants, it is a harsh reminder of how much closer they are to penury. For some, it appears to be a validation of the voices in their heads that they are not good enough.

It does not help that in our climes, many recruiters don't give feedback on the rationale behind their rejection of interviewed candidates. Some even do not communicate at all with their rejected interviewed applicants. This can leave the applicants questioning themselves. 'What did I do wrong?'

It is not unusual to go through this phase, as disappointment is a valid emotion. I have been there before.

Around 2017 0r 2018, having worked with the biggest telecoms company in Africa for only six months, I applied for a job at The Nigerian Stock Exchange. I scaled the two test stages and was invited for an interview. It was the largest panel of interviewers I had ever seen. I sat alone, facing about ten people on the other side of the unusually long table. As if that was not daunting enough, one of the first questions thrown at me was, 'You have all but spent six months in your present company (as stated in my CV); why do you want to leave?'

I was confounded and wondered why they had bothered to invite me for an interview since my short duration at my current job concerned them so much.

I didn't see that first question coming and was overcome with tension, so I could not give a convincing response. I said I was leaving my current job because it didn't align with my future objectives. One of the panellists countered me by saying I would likely also up and leave the stock exchange job after a few months with the excuse that it didn't align with my future objectives. He had a point, and we spent about 15 mins just going on about why I was leaving a place I had barely started in. I was completely demoralised.

By the time the simpler questions came, I was too rattled to answer them correctly. Not surprisingly, I did not get called back after that day, and that interview remains the worst I have had so far in my career.

But I did not let that single bad experience define me. Instead, in my usual fashion of conducting an appraisal of my last interviews, I asked myself what lessons I could learn from my poor performance. **I thought long and hard about how I could have responded to that first interview question in a better way.**

Exactly four weeks after that experience, I got called for another interview that would eventually launch me into my senior management role. The role I had lost was a manager role, so it felt like it was just to prepare me for something bigger in the future. And I was able to land the job.

The first question they asked was the same one I was asked in my interview at the Stock Exchange, but I had reviewed my previous bad experience and prepared a better response. So I answered the question confidently in a completely different manner.

The right mindset to rejection is to remember that it is not a reflection of your worth or abilities. Rather, it is an exposition of the few extra things you ought to learn about the process. Therefore, do not play the blame game, instead, take responsibility always.

Also, if you suspect that your rejection was because of your inability to impress the interviewer on some questions, rather than sulk about the lost opportunity, brush up on your knowledge instead.

There is a lesson to be learnt in every rejection, and you should do well to learn it.

Entry-Level Dos and Don'ts

Many entry-level professionals often find out a little too late that it takes more than technical knowledge to thrive in a work environment. There are certain professional codes of conduct required of entry-level employees, and defaulting on them may negatively affect their relationship with co-workers and, ultimately, their overall work experience.

Here are a few important things you must know as you commence your career journey:

Dos

- **Ask questions**

The entry-level phase is the best period to acquire knowledge in areas where you are lacking. Specifically, in the first six months, ask all the questions and do not be embarrassed to do so. Your colleagues and superiors will most likely be willing to put you through and help you settle in.

If you ask these questions in the first six months, you will be called inquisitive, but if you ask these same questions after twelve months, you will be called incompetent. Therefore it is better you ask them early enough. Asking simple questions like what the company does and several other technical ones will help you better understand your job requirements.

- **Be willing to go the extra mile**

You must come to terms with the truth that you cannot work the same number of hours as your bosses. Most people believe their bosses earn more than them, so they should work longer hours. Smart thinking is: 'if I want to beat their timelines and improve on my deliverables, I will have to put in extra work so that I can be where they are in some years. After all, it took them several years of practice to achieve the efficiency and speed with which they delivered on their tasks.

Working extra hard does not always have to translate to physical exertion. It could also mean spending more time reading and researching. Always remember that the top is not for those who put in the bare minimum effort.

- **Invest in quality relationships**

As long as you aim to go far in your career and have a positive influence, you must not be found in the camp of those whose philosophy about work is simply to show up in the morning, execute their daily deliverables and exit the office without fostering relationships. You need people, and more importantly, you need your bosses. Show genuine interest in them and follow up on their achievements and milestones. Ask if there are certain tasks you can help them with.

Thankfully, the internet has made it much easier to do this. Work- life balance as we know it has been phased out by the COVID-19 pandemic, after all. What obtains today is work-life integration. Therefore, feel free to congratulate your boss on their wedding anniversary or child's birthday. This personal relationship allows you to have 'off work' conversations and build a better friendship with them. This is where sometimes they give you advice and career tips.

Building a personal relationship with your bosses is not synonymous with currying favour or engaging in eye service. But a major rule for succeeding in society is mastering the right social skills. Loners will suffer in today's world.

- **Know where the power lies**

Be aware of the power dynamics in your office. Do not be naïve or listen to those who ignorantly talk about avoiding office politics. Politics manifests anywhere more than one person is present, especially when they come from different backgrounds, hold different perspectives, and have different interests. Learn diplomacy, especially when relating with those who hold the most influence. It will help you a lot as you navigate your job relationships and progress in your career.

Don'ts

- **Do not openly criticise your boss' opinion or decision**

Your boss will not always be right, and your perspectives will not always be in sync. But regardless of how you feel about their position, you should not assert your opinion over theirs. Be mindful of the tone with which you address them when making suggestions or pointing out their errors.

A trick that always works is to acknowledge the admirable or relatable aspects of their opinions or decisions. Then, without being condescending, point out areas you think can be improved upon.

Sell your ideas as suggestions to help the team progress rather than an opportunity to point out your boss' lapses or flaunt your knowledge. And, finally, you must accept that in the long run, they have the final say.

- **Do not abuse access**

I see many entry-level employees do this and would like to believe it is because they genuinely do not know any better. But your workplace might not be so forgiving. As an entry-level professional, you may not be very familiar with organisational structure and how it works. However, the onus is on you to learn so that you do not inadvertently offend your bosses.

- **Do not skip the line**

Regardless of your relationship with bosses higher up on the organogram, do not slight your line manager by skipping them when making requests or giving reports. Remember that they are the ones to give your appraisal at the end of the day.

- **Do not carry on as though you are doing anyone a favour by working with them**

The workplace today has morphed from employer-centric to employee-centric, and this is a welcome development. But as much as this paradigm shift is admirable, as an employee, you should not display an attitude of arrogance no matter how impressive your background or qualifications are.

During the short time I spent at the first place I ever worked, I had a colleague who had committed most of the accounting principles to memory and could sometimes quote them in an intimidating fashion. Somehow, he had issues with his line manager because, rather than face the task given to him to work on, he would try to have an opinion that he pushed until it started affecting team objectives. Because of that, although he was smart, he missed a promotion.

When we got multiple job offers in my early career days, my friends and I would rub it in our potential employers' faces, even though covertly. But that was a move that could backfire. There are chances that your recruiter or employer would get put off by your attitude and relieve you of the job or opportunity as no one likes to be treated as an option.

The employer-employee relationship is a symbiotic one. Just as the company will be better off with you on the team, you, too, will be better off with the opportunities to exercise and hone your skills.

Enough said about landing your first job and being strategic about getting the most out of the entry-level part of your career. In the next part of this book, you will learn how to navigate the career progression path as you move away from being a career newbie. So, let's begin, shall we?

PART II

CAREER PROGRESSION

It is interesting to know that everything around us is constantly growing, whether or not we are aware of or approve of it. This growth may be positive or negative; the same happens with your career. Once you start your career journey, you will continue to grow in some way. However, the 'catch' is in answer to the question – what direction are you progressing?

Your intentionality about growth is a major determining factor of whether you will achieve the right career progression. Leaving everything about your career to chance and luck could make you stalled at a certain career level, grow a negative slope in your career, or leave you at the tail of such a career path.

The point is that anybody can be interested in starting a career, but it takes more than 'being interested' to achieve career progression or even switch paths once you've started your career journey. You may think that being qualified and competent alone should be enough to sustain your career's progress, but it takes more than that to gain tracking and rise to notable heights in your career.

Your progress will often depend on higher levels of decisiveness, intelligence, and humility before you can grow from being an entry- level career person to mid and senior management levels.

And when you discover that you are on the wrong career path, making sudden decisions based on emotions or gratification may be an expensive mistake if your transition is not properly managed and strategic.

In this part, I discuss issues around Changing Career Paths, Office Politics, and Climbing the Career Ladder as means to career progression.

CHAPTER 4

CHANGING CAREER PATHS

The first chapter of this book talked about goals and how they impact choosing a career path. This is pivotal because it sets the base for everything discussed in this chapter and even down the road as you continue your career journey. In the same way, it is necessary to have clear goals and aspirations at the start of your career. It is also important to consider your goals and aspirations before changing career paths.

It is usually difficult to realise that you are on the wrong career path when you do not have a goal or aspiration that you are convinced about.

There is something I find interesting about the UEFA Champions League that aligns with a point I am about to make about career paths. This champions league is a gathering of champions from all European nations. And champions from different European leagues come together to determine who the ultimate champion will be for the whole of Europe.

Now, to get qualified for this competition, each team must have won the championship of their country. That means it would be difficult for a player to aspire to play in or even win the UEFA Champions League if they are playing for a team that has never won the local championship or is fighting against relegation. So ultimately, their path within their local leagues determines if they hit their goals of playing in the championship or not.

However, if your goal as a player is to play in or win the champions league, you must have aligned yourself by playing for a team that wins the local leagues. If you play for a team that usually wins the local league in England, Spain, or Germany, you are gradually getting on the path to playing in and winning the UEFA Champions League. Pathways are just as important as goals because your pathway will lead you to your destination regardless of your goal.

This is much similar to what happens as regards achieving career success. Your choice of career path determines if you'll achieve your goals. You will never arrive at your desired career destination if you are in the wrong lane.

Switching career paths doesn't make any difference for a lazy person. What do I mean? If you are lazy in one career path, changing career paths will not solve your problem or give you different results. For instance, if a person is lazy in Real Estate and they move to Supply Chain Management, they will achieve the same result regardless.

The first thing that needs clarification is this: why are you switching career paths? This is important because, many times, the problem is just the lazy person wanting to try something else that is not as difficult as where they currently are.

How to Change Your Career Path

The first company I worked with after leaving school offered me a role in Finance, and I spent about six months in that role. At that point, I didn't know about credit or debit, but I was extraordinarily diligent in the role. So much so that I got promoted after six months.

But while all this was going on, I knew what my goal was and what path would lead me there, and I didn't get carried away by the illusion that I could rise through the ranks quickly in Finance simply because I scaled the first year. I knew it would fail the test of time.

Regardless of whether I seemed to have started very fast in Finance, it was a matter of time before I would be exposed at the top that a career in Finance was not for me. So I needed to navigate my way back to the path I thought would help me achieve my goal within my time frame.

Here are things to consider when changing career paths:

- **Motive**

Remember how we talked about having the right motive in the first chapter of this book? Well, the same principle applies here. Your motive is one of the very important things to check before changing your career path.

I have noticed, especially in Africa, that we usually conclude too quickly that a particular person is earning more or has more industry achievements because they have chosen a better or easier career path. Therefore, the grass automatically seems greener on the other side, which is not always true. The grass only gets greener on the other person's side when the person takes responsibility for watering it. So do not be envious of another person's 'green grass'.

I know people who travelled abroad and changed career paths after spending ten years on one path. They changed, simply because they saw their friends do so, only to discover that what they were doing in their country was not as relevant in the country they travelled to. Although, some made the same move, and their careers got accelerated.

For instance, if someone has spent 20 to 30 years on a particular career path and suddenly wants to switch to tech because of its success rate, then the person doesn't plan properly. They could be allowing peer pressure to drive them into making a career mistake, as their motive is wrong. So when they start facing challenges in that field, there would be nothing to sustain their drive.

I had people in their 40s and 50s call me recently about this, and when I checked out their motives, it either had to do with their children, some regrets, or a friend doing better. This is why it is important to check your 'why' before you switch career paths.

- **Mentors/Guides**

It is not advisable to change career paths in your late 30s or 40s if you don't have a mentor who can guide you. The truth is, at that point, you do not have much time to dilly-dally. Of course, you also need mentors in your 20s, but there's still time to remediate mistakes at that phase.

However, for someone in their late 30s up to their 50s, it is riskier to take career risks at that point. This is why it is crucial to have a mentor to guide you in the field you want to go into before you leap. I didn't just switch career paths because I felt I could do so. I did it with the guidance of mentors and those who had gone ahead of me and were doing well despite moving from Finance to IT. That was probably why my transition was near seamless.

- **Professional exams**

I believe it is important to take professional exams as you transition to a new career path. And by this, I mean exams that speak to expertise that aligns with the field you are looking to enter. I have eleven professional certifications, and I learned this from one of my mentors, who told me to plan on taking at least one professional exam every year. I have tried to be consistent with it. Now imagine you trying to enter my field and wanting to compete with me without any certifications or years of experience. You will struggle.

Taking professional exams makes you committed to growing in the career path to which you are switching. It challenges you and keeps you focused on what some of the technical knowledge requirements are in the field you desire. For example, if you are looking to switch to finance, you may want to have certifications in Financial Analysis. If it is IT you are looking to switch to – depending on what area you wish to specialise in – you may want to have certifications in Information Technology, Project Management, Product Management, Business Analysis, Information Security, or some other globally recognised certifications.

Doing this exposes you to some of the technical requirements for that discipline and gives you professional validation that you have achieved something before you go into that field – which is good. Does having a certification automatically make you an expert? No, but it does give you leverage.

- **Humility**

This point may not appear important, but I assure you it is. After spending some years in a particular space, switching to a new space will pose challenges since you will most likely start from the rear. This is a reality you will need to embrace.

Someone who wanted to change career paths was in one of my mentorship classes, and he told us how embarrassed he was when he had to learn an accounting course in a South American country. While there, he realised that most of his classmates were in their early 20s since they were fresh from college, and this made him feel embarrassed since he was 48 and was only a beginner on the career path alongside them.

Sometimes, you need to pull back to gain more velocity to move forward faster. If it is a career change you want, then you must be ready to pursue it without shame or pride. After all, pursuit is the evidence of desire.

Smart Transitioning – Managing the Transition

Another factor to consider is what I call 'smart transitioning'. In this context, smart transitioning means how you can manage your transition from one career path to the other in a non-disruptive manner.

Many times, when people try to switch career paths, they want to move from being a marketer for ten years to becoming a tech professional overnight. And the accompanying challenges shuts down the idea in their mind. They get overwhelmed with questions such as: Where do I start from? What do I do first? Then they start applying to companies for jobs in tech without the proper requirements, and no company gets back to them.

Agreeably, transiting from one career to another is not without challenges and can leave you questioning if you can catch up with those ahead of you. So here are some tips for smart transitioning and how to go about it.

- **Leverage your current experience**

When people seek a new job in a new field, they often discard the fact that many of the skills they accumulated in their present profession over the years could be useful. Although you need to identify the new skills you'll need at your new job, you should also consider leveraging your transferable skills.

For instance, you are in the educational field as the head of a department, and you are about to transition to the accounting sector. You certainly have leadership, management, analytical, organisational, and coordinating skills from your previous job that can be transferred to your new job.

Additionally, you can begin to make enquiries and learn more about how the accounts of your department are managed and reported. A little knowledge here and there will make a lot of difference when you eventually transition.

I had a mentee who worked at a multinational with about seven years of experience in Risk Management. She wanted to move over to Supply Chain and just wanted to know how she could make the transition, so I advised her to conduct some research.

Aside from this, there is a module that I usually take my mentees through to extract their motives for career transition. I took her through the module because I needed to know her motive. Was she changing her career path because she needed better pay? Or because she had done an industry trend analysis of her current career path and concluded that, due to technological trends, this career would be extinct in XYZ years? Or was she moving because someone told her to?

She eventually got a role as a Supply Chain Risk Manager. Remember, she was in risk management and was trying to enter Supply Chain. She leveraged her Risk Management expertise for a role in Supply Chain. After a few years, she learned the core business of Supply Chain Management. Today, she is the director of one of the biggest multinationals in Abidjan, and the company runs a balance sheet of billions of dollars.

Smart transitioning requires that you leverage your current role, expertise, and even the company you currently work for. Many people work in a bank with about fifteen to twenty departments; IT, Finance, Payroll, Training, Marketing, Sales, etc. And then you see someone in IT say they are looking for a role in the commercial industry, and they are applying for external positions, forgetting that they can get the role internally.

The smart transition here is, why not make your transition internal? That was exactly what I did.

Here is the summary of my story. I worked in the finance department of a company – a consulting company – for six months. I needed to move to IT because it was in alignment with my career goals.

So, after some months, I tried to transition to IT, but all external vacancy applications I made were rejected. I was fresh out of school, so my only experience was Finance, account preparation, loan monitoring, etc. So, I asked them about the IT arm of the company and if they take people internally, and someone told me yes.

From that point, I kept pestering my Line Manager to take me to the IT department for us to have a conversation. I leveraged the internal mechanism of the company to get me to move over to IT internally. However, of course, I wasn't expecting anyone to jump and give me a promotion within six months. I had to do all the things that I mentioned earlier.

Leveraging your current company is a good way to transition.

- **Research**

Research the industry you want to transition into and familiarise yourself with the knowledge and expectations of the field. Study websites, articles, and other publications of experts in that field. Ultimately, you will discover that you are not the first person trying to transition into that field, and you may also not be the first person transiting from your current field.

The best advice is to study those who have transited from your current field to your desired field. That way, you will have exact and clear steps to follow and the mistakes to avoid. However, suppose you do not find someone who has been able to transition from your present field to the one you desire to go into; in that case, you could read about people who did something similar and follow the principles they applied.

- **Identify the skills you need**

After thoroughly researching your desired field, find out the specific area you want to major in. While at it, do a gap and time assessment to help you know how long you have to get the skills needed for success in the new path to which you are transitioning. Then you can better make an informed decision.

What to Do When You Change Your Career Path

If you are saying to yourself, 'I wish I read this book earlier. I just changed career paths, and maybe my motive wasn't right. What principles can I follow to get ahead in my new field?' The truth is, when it comes to changing your career path, there is no straightjacket way to get it done. How you transition depends on the nature of the career path you are transitioning from and to.

The principles to follow are slightly different from profession to profession. However, some principles have worked for me, and my mentees have also applied the same, and it worked for them. These are the principles I believe you can also follow if you recently changed your career path and are feeling a bit confused.

- **Leverage Senior Industry Colleagues**

Suppose you have newly changed career paths, and you asked me for advice on your next steps; here's the first thing I would tell you: There are always those who have gone ahead of you in any career path you just switched to. You will need to be humble enough to ask them how they do what they do and why it has taken them some years to get where they are. From there, you will begin to learn the next steps from them.

Don't try to be a disruptor. You can only disrupt what you understand. Be willing to learn. I usually advise people to give it six months. Within that time frame, make sure you leverage their guidance, be humble enough to learn, and ask the right questions.

- **Pursue Knowledge**

Read twice as much as those ahead of you. It is always important to know why your colleagues know what they know. In my case, I formed a habit of reading for an hour every day for the last ten years. When I started in IT, my mentors told me that if I read consistently about my chosen career for 30 minutes daily, I would spend half the time others would spend achieving their goals. This has proven to be true. Every day, I wake at 4:30 am and read for an hour. This has brought unfathomable results to my work. I know this because I changed career paths twice – from Finance to IT auditing and then to Cyber security.

I can recall that during the first training I did in Cyber security, the facilitator told my boss then that there was no way I would ever cope with the career path because it was just too technical. As a result, I was not part of the first set of projects the company handled after that training. I understood that those I was to understudy had more technical on-the-job skills than me. I did not try to say, 'What's so special about them? Why do they think I can't do the same?' Instead, I stayed around the team to learn and understudy; I had to work twice as hard to catch up. And today, the story is different.

Fast forward to today, I am seen as a global leader in the cyber security industry. Heiden's magazine in the United States (July 2022 edition) recognised me as Africa's most sought-after cyber security advisor. However, that took a lot of diligent work and consistency.

- **Work Smart**

Another thing to do if you have just changed career paths is to work smart. Like I had said, when you launch into a new career, understand that you will be pushed to the rear of that profession. You don't just work hard but smart.

'Smart' here means reaching out to other professionals outside your organisation. For instance, when I started in cyber security, I met people who could already play with two or more programming languages, while I did not know of any. I had to reach out to someone outside my organisation who began to organise Saturday classes for me.

I began to leverage that knowledge in solving business problems, and people noticed it. Of course, they weren't aware that a couple of things had been happening over the weekend that contributed to my growth.

- **Solve Problems**

When you change your career path or move to a new department, the best way to stand out is to look for long-nagging problems and challenge yourself to solve them. This is how you become almost like a superstar within a short time. Every industry has problems that have not been addressed.

When I moved from Finance to IT, I asked what the problems in the department were, and I was told that one of them was the need to automate some processes around oil and gas. I leveraged the knowledge from my weekend classes to solve the problem. Although it took me nearly a year to solve this problem but guess what? I got a double promotion within that year.

The bottom line is, scan the industry or your company, find out what problems exist, and proffer solutions to them, and you will be celebrated as though you have been in the industry for some time.

As I close out this chapter, I would like to state that accountability is key in everything you do in your career. You need someone to hold you accountable for reading, writing your exams, and solving problems, or you may start with all you've learned easily and then fall off.

Also, whenever you are certain you are on the wrong path – after checking your motives, objectives, and values – do not be afraid to change your career path. Regardless of how fast you go in the wrong direction, you will never arrive at your desired destination. Therefore, ensure you constantly evaluate your progression to ascertain if you are always going in the right direction in your career.

CHAPTER 5

OFFICE POLITICS

Many people have asked me if they need to play office politics to get ahead in the workplace, and I understand the reason behind this question. My answer is always the same: yes, you need to play office politics. What matters, however, is your 'how' and 'why' you play it.

Your **why** matters because, even though you may shy away from office politics out of a sense of moral superiority, what truly confers morality on your actions are the motivations behind them.

Your **how** is equally important because the end does not always justify the means. Especially if you have moral values that you hold dear and you aim to achieve your desires without short-changing others.

But I understand that the idea of competition and powerplay, two inextricable characteristics of office politics, makes many people – and perhaps, even you – uncomfortable. I hope that by the end of this chapter, you will have a good understanding of both and learn to leverage them for your success.

Understanding Powerplay and Competition

Oxford Languages, producers of one of the world's most trusted English dictionaries, defines office politics as 'actions and behaviours involving competition for status or power in a workplace'.

You will notice that in a vacuum, all the words in that definition have no connotation; good or evil. You want to get ahead in your workplace, otherwise, you would not be reading this book. And that is not a bad thing. That is why we all aspire to higher positions at our jobs. Also, we have to compete for these positions because every organisation's organogram is designed to accommodate fewer people at the top positions.

What then describes the kind of politics we play is the behaviour we display and the acts we engage in to achieve our objectives.

Take sports, for instance. Players are heavily penalised when they indulge in harmful acts to get ahead of the competition, like when they take performance-enhancing drugs. However, that penalty is not to punish them for their desire to outperform the opponent because competition is not the problem. But rather, the action they have taken to ensure their success is wrong.

Many people, thinking they are being modest, would often say, 'I'm not a competitive person', but that is not the language of champions. No one who plays or wins the World Cup says they are not competitive. Merely showing up on the pitch means signing up for fierce competition with just one aim: win.

Competition, therefore, is necessary for growth and achievement, and so is politics, especially in the workplace.

What is Bad Office Politics?

Think about all the things you heard about office politics that made you recoil at the thought of engaging in it. Those are bad politics. From my experience dealing with various people in the workplace, I will share some unwholesome attitudes common to those who play bad office politics.

- **They adopt the win-at-all-cost mentality**

Values make a person, and the person who loses their values in pursuit of the world has, in essence, lost it all. People who play bad office politics are either not attentive enough to notice or do not care that their ambition has eroded their value system. They do not hesitate to trade their loyalty or relationships for their pursuit.

Yes, they are driven, but they have no boundaries, no loyalties, and no dos and don'ts driven by values. They sometimes achieve their objective, but with so much collateral damage. The values that direct your life will inform how your winning mentality will play out.

- **They build relationships solely for selfish purposes**

You might know one or two people in your workplace who seem to remember that you exist only when they need something from you that will benefit them. They do not particularly care to know why you were not at work the previous day or care to empathise with your welfare or insecurities. Every piece of information they glean from you is potential ammunition in their arsenal. They report your weakness to the boss and use it to gain an unfair advantage over you. Every time they linger around your workstation to make small talk, you are almost certain that a request will follow shortly after, that day or the next.

These people abuse the essence and purpose of relationships and make it all about themselves. They get close enough to understand your weak points and capitalise on them to get ahead of you.

- **They tell everyone what they want to hear**

To explain this, I'll share the story of one of my mentees who is an assistant manager at her company. One day, she had to wait outside during a board meeting to serve as backup for her senior, the company secretary, who was in the meeting. While waiting outside the boardroom, she received news that her baby was ill and being rushed to the hospital. As she could not reach her boss, who was deeply engaged in the meeting and had to rush off, she pleaded with her colleague to inform her boss about her impromptu exit from duty and the reason for it.

When she resumed work the following day, she met a query awaiting her. She was interrogated for neglecting her duty and going home without permission. Surprised, she called her colleague, whom she had informed about her emergency the previous day. The colleague promised to email the boss to confirm that my mentee had informed her and not simply abandoned her duty post. But she never did.

The next day, when they both stood before the boss and this colleague had yet another opportunity to absolve my mentee of her query, she denied that my mentee had informed her about the emergency. My mentee was both shocked and hurt and almost responded with physical assault.

What that colleague did is typical of people who play bad politics. They appear to empathise with one party in one moment, and the next, they take sides with the other party, especially if it is a higher authority.

- **They engage in 'eye service'**

Diligence is a great strategy for playing office politics, but people who play bad politics put in the required effort on their duties only when they are being watched. They are the type that closes late when the boss is around, but leave shortly after the boss does.

They dress smartly and in line with the company's dress code when the boss is around, but otherwise, they dress and act as they like. They appear extra tired and always want to make it obvious to everyone, especially the bosses, that they have worked harder than others.

- **They sabotage the efforts of others to reach their height**

Imagine someone climbing up a ladder to reach the top and then kicking the ladder away after achieving their aim so that no one else can get to the top. This situation can be complicated because people who do this often act like they are not aware of their actions and the implications.

Very early in my career, I once had a superior expecting to be promoted to manager. He told me and a few others about how he was about to be denied the role despite his glaring capability because his years of experience did not match the company's requirements. That made no sense to us. Eventually, some people advocated for him, and he got the promotion.

Three years later, I was in the same situation. But this same superior told me that, although he knew my performance was even more exceptional than my close competitors', he would choose them over me because they had more years of experience than I did. The sheer irony!

He seemed keener on establishing a reputation as the only one to break the record of becoming a manager in only a few years. He would not allow me to get such privilege and the improved social capital accrued to it, so he resorted to sabotaging my growth within the company.

People like that always hide their bad office politics with terms such as 'due process', 'discipline', or 'this is beyond me'. And unless you are self-aware, you may not easily detect that their actions are motivated by their selfish interests and not by the 'pristine' values they claim to live by.

What to do when you're a victim of Bad Office Politics

- **Do not act based on instincts**

Recall the story of my mentee whose colleague denied her before the boss. She almost hit her colleague out of shock and disgust at her blatant dishonesty. While it might be tempting to rationalise her outburst, I must say that such a response is a bad idea and can lead to many adverse consequences for you and your career.

When you find yourself at the receiving end of bad office politics, be careful not to act on your instinct. You might be tempted to send your aggressor a stinker, but don't. Do not send a long email complaining to your boss about how you have been wonderful and yet he has been victimising you. Do not raise a voice at your boss.

In other words, swallow your first reaction.

- **Evaluate the role you might have played in the situation**

Many people who claim to be victims are simply getting the reward for their poor-quality work. When it seems that others have been favoured over you, the best attitude is to engage in some introspection. Do you hit your targets as they do? Could it be that they are being compensated for the extra efforts that they put in, which you don't?

I once worked in a company with an HR manager who constantly complained of victimisation. Even when the head of HR was changed, her complaint persisted. I had to get her to reorientate her mindset. She was not being targeted in any way; she simply needed to take more responsibility for her job.

Always check with objectivity that you are not the one with the problem because if you are comfortable with underperformance, even the best office politics will work against you.

- **Engage in a polite conversation to find out what the problem is**

Stephen R. Covey recommends in one of his books, *The 7 Habits of Highly Effective People*, 'Seek first to understand, then to be understood'. You may find a situation or piece of information appalling but do not set out to address it while you are in a fit. Try to understand the rationale behind the actions or decisions, no matter how detrimental they seem to your interest.

Realising I could not be promoted for no other reason than my years of experience, I did not necessarily agree with my boss's decision. Still, I knew what the issue was, and it was clear to me the next steps I needed to take.

- **Walk the legal channels**

Find out from the HR officer attached to your department if there is a grievance process you can work through. There are legal processes ensuring you get fair treatment in your company so that you can continue to deliver on your job with a sense of purpose and satisfaction. Be sure to take advantage of these channels.

- **Talk to a senior colleague within the organisation**

I believe that no matter how many people within your organisation work against you, there has to be a superior that you can talk to. For example, one of my mentees, working in the same company where I was working, was having a difficult time with her boss. I was privy to this because I'd mentored her for close to seven years, so I knew her career story.

As I was a senior and on the same level as the boss who was giving her a hard time, I was able to convince other people in the company who mattered to hear her side of the story objectively. We walked her through the legal channels, and ultimately, the boss was asked to leave because he had contravened so many company policies and was simply a bully.

Situations like this are why it is important to have people who can talk about your good works and leverage other relationships to your advantage in the company.

- **Have professional visibility outside your organisation**

Regardless of your level of competence at your job, when you remain unknown outside the four walls of your organisation, it will be difficult for you to quit as urgently as you desire if you are being victimised or unappreciated. The solution is to build a strong professional reputation in your industry. When your bosses are aware of this, and when they see for themselves how customers or competitors try to poach you, it is unlikely that they will ever take you for granted.

What Is Good Office Politics, and How Do You Leverage It for Career Growth?

Unlike bad office politics where people play to win at all costs, in good office politics, you simply play to win. There is a difference between a winning mentality and a win-at-all-cost mentality. While one is guided by values and principles, the other is not.

The mind is such a powerful tool; the moment you set your mind to win and block out all negative options like bribery, backbiting, sabotage, and other vices, you begin to see credible ways of winning. The following are my suggestions for leveraging good office politics:

- **Be the undeniable best at what you do**

This is the winning mentality. If everyone can agree that you excel at what you do, that would be your first step to playing good office politics. I call it the first step because, sometimes, the reward of your genius will not come to you on a silver platter. You will have to market it to the right people so that they can see and understand the value you bring.

- **Create relationships**

Unlike in bad office politics, where relationships are built simply with the ulterior motive of using people, in good politics, relationships are developed mainly for the purpose of genuine friendships. I always define genuine friendship or relationship as a mutually beneficial social contract or a value-for-value exchange. It is not an opportunistic use-and-discard arrangement.

I recall one of the relationships that greatly helped me to date. I tried to build a relationship with the senior manager in one of the places where I once worked. She was feared by most because of her attention to detail and strict demands for excellence. With lots of intentional and genuine efforts on my part, I succeeded in making her acquaintance. Then one day, she looked at me and said, 'Hey, I really think you can be on the ISACA board'.

ISACA is the biggest international body for IT governance and IT security professionals in the world, and at that time, I had all but three years of experience. At this time, the people on the board had been in the industry for decades. On the other hand, I was only in my twenties, yet my senior manager would not stop pushing me. She was also a board member. She gave me all the support and encouragement I needed, and eventually, I made it to that board; in fact, I was the youngest member. I doubt that I would have been able to achieve that had I not built a solid relationship with her and if she hadn't seen me as competent.

- **Pay attention to how your bosses like their deliverables**

Your ability to understand your boss and give them their deliverables how they want is one good way to stand out among your peers and get the boss on your side. Some bosses get upset when reports are submitted with font types and sizes that they do not approve of. Some favour certain writing tones and styles over others. Some do not like receiving any job deliverables over the weekend, while others immensely appreciate subordinates who do so as it shows the employee is going the extra mile.

I once had a boss who often sent his reviews and comments to the team around 4:30 a.m. to 6:00 a.m. This boss was about three to four steps my senior on the career ladder, and ordinarily, I had no cause or opportunity to interact with him. So, I reasoned that if I could acknowledge the receipt of his reports (with a little appreciation) within the time frame he sent them, I would gain a better audience with him. I did just that.

One random day, he commented about my dependable availability whenever he sent me materials. Even though I was not immediately aware of it, the man had noticed me. He asked why I was always on hand to respond in those early hours, and I told him that that was when I did my reading. That was one of the ways I won his attention and respect that created a perception immediately.

- **Strategically sell yourself**

In any workplace, you will find empty barrels that make the loudest noise, people who are light but hide under a bushel, and those extraordinary performers who strategically sell themselves. The third category is where you ought to be.

You must be conscious about your environment enough to know those who make the decisions. Identify the final consumers of your extraordinary deliverables and find a way to tell them that you were the brain behind them. There is no point in being a star under a stool, nor is there any value in selling yourself short.

- **Show appreciation**

This is a bit tricky because it could be labelled bribery or corruption, depending on the prism from which it is viewed. Trying to avoid this, some people veer towards the extreme.

At one of the places where I worked previously, I always sent a thank-you message to my bosses after receiving a promotion or an annual bonus. On the other hand, some of my colleagues insisted that they owed no one any appreciation since they got what they got by merit. But I had a different perspective. I have noticed from personal experience that showing gratitude gives you a world of good.

I am not suggesting you buy your boss a car because you got promoted. Often, a simple 'thank you,' to acknowledge their endorsement of you can communicate that you are a grateful person, even with no money or gift exchanging hands.

- **Help your team members shine**

Always remember that for people who play good office politics, the goal is to win and not to win at the expense of others. If you have benefited from an opportunity or privilege, do well to pay it forward. You deserve to build your career in a healthy work environment. Help foster this by creating a pathway for others to achieve as much success as you have.

CHAPTER 6

CLIMBING THE LADDER

I am about to take you on yet another ride full of lessons I learned in my progression from entry-level to mid-management, senior management, and executive-level management. I'll share my personal experience, and I hope this helps you through your journey.

I spent six years from being a fresh university graduate to becoming a manager; eight months from a manager to a senior manager; two years from a senior manager to an associate director; and ten months from an associate director to a director.

This happened across three different multinational companies. As you've known from the previous chapters, I switched companies, and one of the things I'll discuss here is when to change companies and leverage that change for career acceleration.

You may wonder, 'Is it possible to have a rapidly accelerated career in the same company?' Maybe. Although that wasn't my experience, it could be possible for someone else. You would notice I had my longest stretch from entry-level to managerial level. I believe if I had read a book like this back then, it would have taken a shorter time.

Some people may think that spending zero to six years from being a fresh graduate to becoming a manager in a multinational company is fast, some may think it is okay, while others may consider it slow. But in the context of this book, I would say it could have been faster. I hope you can utilise what you learn from this book to make your progression faster.

Why did my acceleration increase in the following years after becoming a manager?

I simply learned from the mistakes I made in my first six years and the principles I never understood nor engaged in consciously before. It is possible to unconsciously engage some principles and achieve results without necessarily understanding them, so I learned to engage those principles actively and leverage them. I also spent more time reading and, of course, networking.

Moving to Mid-Level Management

Based on my personal experience and that of the people I have mentored who have achieved desirable results, I will mention some skills and habits that helped to achieve these results. They are specifically behavioural and technical.

- **Have a sharp learning curve**

A learning curve is the rate of a person's progress in gaining experience or new skills. Having a sharp learning curve means the rate at which you acquire the needful experience and understanding for your core deliverables needs to be very fast if you want to move quickly into mid-level management.

It also means you can't put the same amount of work, effort, and time into gaining skills as the average person; you will have to do more. In my case, I had to spend some weekends learning the required skills. The faster you can turn your curve, the faster you begin to make a push to mid-management.

- **Be a subject matter expert in your field**

One of the things you must do when trying to move to mid-level management is to be so good at what you do that your results become glaring. There must be certain technical requirements in your field that will make you the go-to person in your function or department.

In a regular organogram in most organisations, the bottom of the pyramid – where the entry-level belongs – has the largest number of people, making it the most difficult place to stand out. Nevertheless, one way to truly stand out is to be a 'solutions provider' to technical problems in your organisation.

One of the interesting things that happened in a company I worked for was that there were issues with performing proper data analysis. I identified that as a potential opportunity and began to invest my time in acquiring the necessary knowledge to become an expert in using a data analysis tool in a few months. Subsequently, I began to use this tool to analyse many long-standing data problems at that company.

It was a consulting company, and the staff usually performed various tasks at various locations. So, when everyone went to their clients and came back with complex data that needed to be analysed, I was the person they came to. My colleagues and bosses began to say, 'Reach out to Fene if you have this problem'. That is simply a way to build credibility in an area of expertise.

- **Beat your timelines**

There are three types of people in this context:

1. Those who miss timelines.
2. Those who meet timelines.
3. Those who beat timelines.

Having a timeline means you have to deliver before the expected time, and because you are a subject matter expert, you must not compromise quality. For instance, if you promise your boss to deliver a certain assignment on Thursday and you deliver on Wednesday, your boss will gradually begin to see you as a reliable employee, especially if you do this consistently.

I can't remember not meeting a deadline set by any of my bosses in the last seven years of my career.

- **Be consistent**

Consistency is closely tied to timeline and is essential in moving to mid-level management. Good quality work today and poor quality work tomorrow will make you forgettable.

One of the things that helped me move up quickly is consistency. I made sure I was consistent in my deliveries.

Consistency brings confidence. The major reason you would be considered an expert in that particular field is that every time you have been assigned any project, you consistently deliver with exceptional quality.

Remember that from entry-level up to your first five years, you must find ways to stand out. Consistency separates you from the crowd.

- **Be friends with the managers**

One of the things to do when you want to move quickly into mid- management is to know what your managers are doing and what the expectation is on that level you desire.

Most times, people wrongly assume and say things like, 'What are they doing that I can't do?' Well, you need to find out what your managers engage in.

This helped me greatly because I didn't just assume I had the skill for the next level; I kept asking for the skills required. This kind of conversation with a boss can only happen if you are friends, as they do not owe you such.

I also learned that the managers in my workplace were doing more than just ensuring technical delivery from projects. They monitored how we managed our time, how we billed the customers, etc. When you know what they do and the required skills, you'll suddenly begin to gain perspective and align your work with it.

- **Look for problem areas that others are avoiding**

This is your biggest opportunity when seeking to move into middle management because rewards are often tied to problem-solving. Something only remains a problem when people avoid it or do not have the right resources or skills to solve it.

Be the brave one, and step out to solve it. Although it looks like an easy way to jump higher, it isn't necessarily. I have leveraged this consistently, even at the executive management level. But there is a flip side – if you fail at solving that problem, you could be labelled. *But hey, what if you succeed?* That should be your mentality.

As a subject matter expert, you should be willing to solve outstanding business issues in your department that others may be trying to avoid.

Moving to Senior-Level Management

As a middle-level manager who wants to move to senior-level management, you should consider these things:

- **Understand what makes the bottom line of your company**

This simply means you need to understand how the company makes money. It is easier to figure this out if you are in certain functions such as Finance, Treasury, Revenue Assurance, etc. It's also easy to articulate how the company makes money if you work in marketing and sales because you are a part of that process on the front line, and you could easily tie your daily task to the bottom line.

However, it is a lot more difficult for unrelated fields because you are an enabler of the business or a support function. You could get lost in doing several operational activities, which is what people in mid-level management and lower levels do.

Many get too tied to administrative and daily tasks, forgetting there is a bigger picture. However, if you are considering moving to senior management, you need to be curious about how your salary gets paid.

One of the things that helped me was finding out how I connected to the bottom line, so that perspective enhanced how I solved problems at work.

There are several problems in various companies, especially in multinationals. You need to articulate the specific one to solve that will have a direct bottom-line impact. This can only be done when there's a proper understanding of how your work relates to the bottom line.

Like I did, sometimes you may need to step out of your department to solve a problem that has a larger business impact. And of which you have the skill to achieve the required result.

- **Understand what your senior manager wants**

I learned a long time ago that 'good' has different flavours. For instance, ice cream is fundamentally sweet but has different flavours. Some people like vanilla, some chocolate, some strawberry, and some love the several new flavours that have been developed.

If you want to move from mid-management to senior management, you need to know that for senior managers, 'good' comes to them in various flavours.

One of the things I did when I took up the role of a manager in a publicly listed company was to sit with my senior manager and ask several questions. Some of the questions I asked were: What are your preferred ways of working? Are you just result-oriented, or do you want to be taken along on a task-by-task basis? Can I take full responsibility for the team?

Some senior managers will give you a task and a timeline and then wait for you when it's time to deliver. While some want daily, weekly, or hourly updates, none is right or wrong. It is simply their preference. As a manager, emotional intelligence suggests that you understand what your senior manager wants.

When I asked my senior manager those questions, my objective was to understand his methods and expectations. I did not assume that I knew what he wanted; instead, I asked and clarified. It took about a week of having several meetings to get clarity on the requests I made, but once that was clear, I mapped out my plans and exceeded the set expectations.

Therefore, it is important to know your senior manager's flavour and give your work to them in that same flavour. Do not try to force them to like yours. That could lead to frustration sometimes, and they could interpret it as your unwillingness to adapt.

- **Learn time management**

The manager level is very dicey because you are expected to deliver on a more technical scale; you are also expected to have some soft skills and to deliver consistent results. Therefore time management is important if you want to handle all your responsibilities. Remember your KPIs are no longer solely based on technical delivery at this stage. Manage your time effectively; understand what is a priority and what isn't.

I constantly engaged Eisenhower's important principles, and it helped.

Also, learn to delegate tasks where necessary and ensure you align with your boss while prioritising.

- **Understand the politics of your environment**

Understanding who the influencers are, who the decision-makers are, and who the noisemakers are, is core at this point.

Is your boss in the right standing with management? If your boss has been out of favour with the senior management, it might be difficult for promotions to come to your team. It's also possible that your team might no longer be aligned with the objectives of senior management.

Although this could result from ignorance on your boss' end, the effects of such misalignment cascade down to the team. and you will notice your team seems to be side-lined or not enjoying the kind of benefits or visibility as other teams do.

Therefore, it is important to know if all you are doing as a team is seen as valuable or not. Ask your boss questions such as: How was the management meeting?

Did you present what we did? What was the feedback? Did the chief financial officer like it?

When you continuously get feedback such as 'they don't value our work', 'they don't understand the value we bring' and 'there wasn't enough time for me to present', that's a red flag for the team.

There are certain individuals you will need to make an effort to show the kind of value you are adding to your company. They need to see the quality of your work.

It is important to consider these as you plan on going into senior management. I know this may not be conventional, but these are practical things I have seen that worked.

I have seen an entire function of over fifty staff being asked to leave a multimillion-dollar company simply because their bosses had driven the team in the opposite direction of the company's objectives for months.

- **Build strategic relationships within the company**

I constantly tell people, 'When it's time to move from a manager to a senior manager, your line manager cannot be the only person that knows you are exceptional at what you do'.

There need to be at least four or five people in senior management that you have been intentionally visible to with the output and quality of your work. They must be able to sing the same song about you as your manager does because it's easy for anyone's line manager to propose a promotion for their subordinates, which could be for various reasons. But when the reasons are not based on empirical evidence from consistent performance of being a high flyer, it is usually due to personal or unprofessional reasons that other managers will unanimously agree to promote someone.

Moving to Executive Management

It took me about two years to move from senior to executive management. First, you need to have a relationship with your company's executive management. They must know your name.

Remember, at this stage, you are getting to the very thin point of your organisation's organogram. This is the level where everyone knows each other, so it's a very close circle you are attempting to break into. As a senior manager, you need to start creating relationships and partnerships with people in executive management.

Most times, when a new director comes into the company, there's usually an announcement, and I would respond to that message by welcoming that person. It's a conversation starter that helps me to get to know the person. If the person were a Muslim, I would send them a felicitation message during their holidays. I also did the same during the Christian holidays.

Ultimately, it's an opportunity to open channels to a relationship. I was not trying to get unnecessary or cheap popularity; I was trying to create a channel for relationships.

I would send birthday messages once a year because I realised that these moments matter in these executives' lives.

Sometimes, when I send those messages, I receive a reply like, 'How are you doing, and how is work?' I would mention in my response how I had just done something that I know is tied to the company's objectives. I usually got an immediate thank you message from them.

Although I may not hear from that person again for some months, an impression has been created, such that whenever they hear my name, they relate it to competence.

That's one way to build strategic relationships with executive management in the office. A time will come when you will need them as you move to a higher level in your career.

What will you tell your CEO, Director, or Chief, if they send you a message asking what you have been doing? You need to prepare for such and have an answer at your fingertips.

- **Develop exceptional presentation skills**

You must be able to handle business presentations that pass across certain thoughts, influence cultures, and are meant to sell what you are doing or reveal your expertise.

One of my bosses was invited to speak at a school recognised as one of the best universities in Nigeria. He was to make a presentation at their Computer Science awareness week, but he couldn't make it, so he decided to send me.

After the presentation, the feedback was so massive that the university wrote a letter to my company saying, 'This is an exceptional talent'. They reported how the students didn't want me to leave and that three representatives from three other universities demanded I come to their institutions to make a similar presentation. I had pushed the name of the company out there in a positive light.

Now, when that sort of feedback goes to your management, what impression do you think that creates for you? Therefore, strong presentation skills are important.

- **Tie your deliverables to the organisational goal**

At this point, the output of your work can no longer be in isolation from the organisational goals and objectives. The organisation's goal must solely become your goal in all your deliveries.

Constantly envision what more you can do to help your company achieve its targets. The more you do this, the closer you get to yours.

- **Have a very strong eye for recruiting the right talent into the company**

This greatly helped me as I only recruited exceptional people. Although, I never knew I was being watched until my boss mentioned it to me when he talked about the things he had to include in my justification for a promotion.

You must ensure that the talent pipeline of your company stays very healthy. If there is always a behavioural or cultural misfit; or technical incompetence among your recruits, I'm sorry, you cannot move to the executive management level.

- **Industry relevance**

Companies love when the people stepping into executive management are respected in the industries they play in. It helps with credibility and gives you a broader view beyond the four walls of your company.

Value for industry relevance weighs more depending on your sector. For example, it is a must-have in professional consulting but not so much in some other sectors. The bottom line is it is an added advantage.

Deciding When to Switch Companies

People always ask me when and why they should change their jobs. I hear things like, 'Is it a good time to change?', 'I'm tired, and I want to move!'

Now, understand that there's no problem working for one company throughout your career. If it gives you fulfilment and aligns with your goals and timeline, then yes, go ahead.

I changed jobs three times in my career, and those I've mentored personally have also changed a few times, but the most important thing to remember when planning to change a job is your motive, which we have discussed before. Your 'why' must be strong; it simply can't be because you want to earn more. While this is an understandable reason, it cannot be the only driver to make a change.

Remember, the grass on the other side is always greener until you get there. Many people I have seen and mentored have fallen victim to this. They leave for another company for higher pay, get there and lose their jobs in three months.

So, there are many other things to consider before making such a move. Things such as the company's culture, sustainability, asset base, and the industry they play in. How relevant will they be in a couple of years due to the kind of business they are into?

What to Consider Before Changing Jobs

When exactly should you contemplate making a switch? I believe it's when you are not making progress in your present place.

Progress here is a forward or onward movement toward a destination.

When my mentees announce that it's time to go because they are not making progress, I always ask, 'What is your destination?' Because it's difficult to talk about progress in the isolation of a destination.

People have changed jobs because they weren't making progress, but some of those moves turned out to be retrogressive. That is why I have previously discussed goal setting. When you set your goals right, your destination will be known. However, it is time to begin looking for a change if you have done your assessment and think you are not making progress.

The next thing you should look out for is when your job begins to affect your personal life and the values you hold dear; then, you should start thinking of making a switch.

I had a mentee who had a new manager; this was post-covid 19, and many Nursery Schools closed by 3 pm, which was earlier than usual. So no one could leave their kids in school till 6 pm anymore. Unfortunately, my mentee still had to close from work by 5 pm because her manager insisted that she couldn't close by 3 pm. The school would call her several times, and soon enough, she began to pay fines. Still, her line manager insisted that she leave by 5 pm even though she would get home to continue working remotely to finish her tasks.

This disruption made her realise it was time for a change because it began to affect her children, and no good parent ever wants that. As you can see, this wasn't because she was lazy but because she was kept in a difficult spot.

Another thing to watch is when your job conversations are always filled with complaints. This will begin to affect your mental health at a point. You will always grumble and stay unhappy since you spend most of your days at work. Soon, the negativity will also begin to influence your effectiveness and productivity, which may lead to an unhealthy downturn. At this juncture, it's time for a change.

Furthermore, when the structures and goals of a company no longer align with your goal, you may need to switch. For instance, when your company comes up with new policies that don't align with your career goals.

I left one of the places I previously worked because my goals suddenly did not align with the organisation. They changed from promoting people every year to promoting every two or three years. As soon as that change happened, among other things, it was clear that I needed a different vehicle to my destination.

Imagine someone who has worked hard for three years and is excited to get a promotion. Only to get served with the news that a new policy had been established that would disrupt it, such as the company's structure becoming flat and promotions getting delayed for the next four years or even completely stopped.

I found out in one of the places I worked that some people had been in the same role for ten years. That was disturbing. My goal was not a salary increment or to hedge against yearly inflation but to attain a certain height in my career at a specific age and time, which did not align with what I discovered there.

These are a few things I have learned in my journey that one should always check. As I have established, the company's vision and structure are extremely important.

One mistake many make at this point of critical change is getting unverified information from ex-staffs of the company they wish to enter. The general reality about staff leaving jobs is that some leave sad while others leave happy, so you could get a biased view of a company if you ask someone who left out of anger or frustration.

I know someone who was about to reject an offer based on a total misrepresentation from an ex-staff of the company, not knowing that that ex-staff was about to reapply for the same role at the same company. The company he had moved to was about to be shut down. If that person had taken that advice, he would never have known that the person he reached out to was untrustworthy, and he would have gotten the wrong impression about the company. What saved him was his communication with a staff that was doing well at that company and who gave him a balanced opinion.

As additional advice, you should ask for the organogram of the company you join; seek to know how many steps you are from the CEO. This is something I always look out for. Be inquisitive; ask how many listed KPIs are expected and ask what career progression opportunities are available.

Finally, ensure that you speak with a mentor. Always carry a mentor along through your career journey.

PART III

RETIREMENT

Not so many career people think much about retirement while they are still young. They believe it is something that should be given attention when they are in their late forties or early fifties. Similarly, career people are known to be so invested in their work that they do not take the issue of becoming an authority in their field seriously.

After you might have stayed and grown in the career path you find most fulfilling and rewarding, it is only wise to firmly establish your presence in your industry and also prepare for retirement.

Regardless of your age and years of experience, you too can carve a niche for yourself and become a force to reckon with not only within the company you work for, but also within the industry and ecosystem of your profession.

Becoming a distinguished and highly respected industry expert does not happen overnight. It is a result of consistency and excellence. It is not essentially tied to just how long you have spent in your industry or how popular you are. Instead, it stems from being a person of substance whose reputation for professionalism and excellence is distinct.

But how do you become that person at a younger age? How do you leverage your current expertise and knowledge of your job and industry? What smart decisions do you need to make in planning for retirement and becoming an authority at a younger age?

I have answered these questions in this part. Read on to learn about Becoming an Authority and Planning for Retirement based on what I did in my thirties and currently do.

I have a piece of advice for you as you leaf through the pages ahead, though: be open-minded. Some new truths you encounter may challenge your long-held beliefs and habits and place more burden of change and proactiveness on you than you are used to. But you can rest assured that you are not alone on this journey.

CHAPTER 7

BECOMING AN AUTHORITY

As we gradually begin to wind down our discussion on career acceleration, it is important to talk about being an authority –

or what some people call a 'thought leader' – in your industry. And as I have consistently done in the course of this book, I will be using myself and my experiences as a practical example.

Who Is a Thought Leader?

A thought leader is someone who offers unique guidance and perspective, inspires innovation, and influences others based on their expertise and perspective in an industry.

So far, I have been privileged to speak at major tech cybersecurity conferences in Africa, the Middle East, and, recently, Europe. I've also been accepted into the Forbes Technology Council, an invitation-only tech council for the top technology executives in the world. Fortunately, I'm one of the few to make it there in their thirties.

In the last two years, I've spoken at over forty-three international conferences and received several awards in the industry. I also mentor over a hundred career professionals. That is what thought leadership is about — being recognised and sought after by your industry. This comes with certain influences and responsibilities.

Regardless of your field, you can (and you should) aspire to thought leadership. But aside from aspiring, it is also important to understand the attributes unique to thought leaders so you are clear on the type of skills and values to imbibe.

Here are a few that I have observed over the years:

- **Deep expertise**

Thought leaders are not shallow in their thinking. Every discussion with them relating to their area of expertise exposes you to new knowledge, and their contributions are full of depth.

This implies that you cannot aspire to thought leadership when you do not consistently spend time reading, researching, and gaining new insights into your industry or area of influence.

- **Unique perspectives**

Their thoughts are not basic, and this is because they are constantly learning and unlearning. Thought leaders are pacesetters; they set standards in the industry that you envy and want to emulate.

- **Strong communication skills**

Thoughts leaders have mastered the art of relating their thoughts through writing and public presentation. They write engaging articles and books and demonstrate powerful presentation skills at conferences, webinars, or other avenues to share their thoughts.

You cannot call yourself a thought leader if you have not given webinars or spoken at major conferences where your industry leaders gather.

- **Industry testaments and high industry visibility**

Industry testaments are those who can say of another career professional, 'S0-and-so held me from Point Zero to Point X; they gave me the opportunity to accomplish this', 'When I listened to this person and applied what they said, I achieved this', or 'This person put in a good word for me with so-and-so, and that is why I have this job'.

Thought leaders are authorities in their industries and can use their influence to create opportunities for others, thereby having industry testaments. High industry visibility means that the names of these people are known within the industry where they operate. They are known and respected by their industry peers.

Now that we have established the attributes common to thought leadership, you may think, 'I know I should be a thought leader, an authority in my field, but nobody knows me. No one invites me for conferences'. You may even be thinking that, perhaps, your boss is only being invited because he carries a big title in the company.

I have been there. I once felt the same way. And I can tell you that when I started speaking on the international stage, it was not because I'd gotten a great title in addition to my name. It was because I had built a track record and portfolio over time. So it did not happen overnight.

The tough truth is that everybody wants what everybody wants, and nobody wants what no one else demands.

Are you interested in moving from industry irrelevance to industry leadership? Below are some practical suggestions based on my experiences.

- **You must have the desire and discipline for it**

As I've done several times in this book, let me reiterate that pursuit is proof of desire. Like anyone else, you can desire to be a thought leader or an authority in your field. But what steps will you be taking to ensure that happens? How much staying power do you have for when you get rejected from various conferences you apply to?

You will have to keep pushing. Your desire for industry relevance must be stronger than the frustration of not getting invited to conferences or not finding a platform to announce yourself, no matter how long you keep trying.

Also, be disciplined enough to give it what it takes—not your best, as your best may not be good enough. Lack of discipline is why people falter just days after their New Year's resolution; they cannot follow through on their desires despite challenges.

- **Look for opportunities to volunteer**

My experience in general, national, and even international conference speaking started with me assisting my boss as a fresh graduate with about two years of experience. Back then, I would offer to write his articles and prepare his slides for his upcoming presentations.

Those slides of mine were, most times, a complete travesty, and he never used them. But I made sure to get the final copies from him always. As for the articles I wrote for him, he signed them off in his name, but I never felt he was doing me any disservice. Rather, I was happy to be part of the learning process.

As time passed, I began to accompany him to events, offering to handle logistics or technical issues with the projector and similar tasks. I was happy to sit and listen. During that period, I discovered something began to happen to my mind as I listened. I started seeing new possibilities, like, *I can speak on this stage, these people are flesh and blood like me, just masters of their discipline*, and so on.

As you hear other speakers address the audience, you get to notice and learn from their speaking styles. I now pay that good experience forward to my mentees. I never go to any conferences or speaking engagements alone. Rather, I always have with me a mentee who is willing to learn and absorb. After the conference, I would ask questions like, 'What did you learn from X and Y's presentation style?' and 'Did you see how this person prepared their slides and how not to?'

- **Prepare for your opportunity before it comes**

Today I can speak to hundreds and even thousands of people. But I started by speaking in front of my mirror and one or two friends before I ever had the opportunity to speak at a conference. I was building confidence and learning how to be eloquent during those times and when the opportunity finally came, I was ready and grabbed it. But how did this opportunity present itself?

I narrated in a previous chapter how I gave a remarkable speech at a university on behalf of my boss. He was the president of an association under which I'd been serving. He couldn't make it to the event, so he asked if I could go on his behalf.

I could have messed up that opportunity in two ways. I could have declined it with the excuse that his request came under short notice (which would mean I was never ready for that opportunity). Or feel offended that he was sending me off to a university and turn down the request. After all, if the event were to involve a multinational, he would clear his schedule to be there.

I didn't do any of those things. Instead, I grabbed the opportunity and went to deliver the speech. The feedback that trailed my speech at the end of the day was that I was extremely talented and that they saw me going places. That event opened the door to three other speaking engagements immediately.

This, dear reader, is what I mean when I say that you must prepare for opportunities and grab them when they arise.

- **Be humble enough to ask**

Many people feel entitled and think, 'I'm a senior manager; they should be the ones reaching out to me for conferences instead', or 'I have ten years of experience in this industry; I should not be begging for conferences'. Other times, hubris rears its insidious head, making them go, 'I have been at senior-level management for the past fifteen years. I do not need to speak to any of the people I see on these platforms'.

Perhaps you may have even attended some conferences and equated yourself with the speaker on the platform, concluding that 'What he just said is common, there's no big deal in his address. I know more than he does'. But the truth is that if you were as visible as the speaker, you would probably be on the same stage too.

You must be humble. Humble enough to ask for opportunities and humble to learn from those who have those opportunities you desire.

- **Check online and do your research**

Many conferences make call-for-speaker announcements. If you do proper research, you'll find some of them and be able to apply for them. I filled out at least fifteen to twenty call-for-speaker application forms before getting a response which was not even favourable. But the day I received that rejection mail, I was elated that, finally, somebody had deigned to respond to me.

Although I publish articles on Forbes today, I didn't start this big. I faced my fair share of rejections, but now I struggle to honour many industry invitations.

The Role of Mentorship in Becoming an Authority

The next thing to do to become a thought leader is to get a mentor. In this section, I will take my time to expound on the importance of mentorship.

What will a mentor do for you?

The first thing a mentor will do for you is they will grant you access. Recall that my first speaking opportunity came up because someone I looked up to was unavailable to attend his speaking engagement, and he decided to hand the opportunity to me, which did big things for my career. The second time I had the privilege to speak at a conference was because another mentor gave me access. He was supposed to speak for twenty minutes, but he graciously gave up the last ten minutes of his time for me to do a demonstration. This is how mentors grant you access.

Secondly, in becoming an authority, mentors shorten your journey. As they have travelled the road before, taking several years to become an authority, get speaking engagements, and get the industry to recognise them, they are able to recommend more efficient hacks and shorter routes to attain their level. And that is the same thing I do now.

I have courses on my website where you can sign up and learn exactly what to do to shorten your journey in a few steps. I have mentees with just three to four years of career experience who have started speaking at conferences they were sourced for, not 'mistaken speakers' like my first opportunity.

I never had that chance. Every other thing I learned before then, I had to figure out on my own. This does not have to be your experience. Get help.

Thirdly, mentors help you to reduce your mistakes. Being a thought leader comes with its own challenges as, to a large extent, you are in the public eye. Your thoughts will be challenged at some conferences; people will ask questions that you never saw coming. Some of these questions are with the sole aim of embarrassing, intimidating, or demystifying you — to prove that you are just as random as everyone else in the room. A mentor teaches you how to handle tough audiences like that.

My mentor was of immense help to me in this regard. He explained the "parking lot" concept to me. He taught me when to take questions to the parking lot and when to bring them out of the parking lot during a presentation. These things are best learnt from mentors because if you wait to learn from your own experience, you would have failed first before beginning to learn the ropes again.

Despite the obvious benefits of mentorship, I have found, in my experience, a few reasons why people do not want to be mentored. The first of these reasons is what I call the proximity syndrome. Some people have the unusual advantage of being close to great minds, but because their closeness grants them a front-row view of the struggles and weaknesses of those great people, they undervalue them.

Because they see the public figure every day, perhaps as their colleague, reporting line, or line manager, they wonder why people adore them, demand their services, or regard them as industry leaders. This is how proximity makes them look down on their potential mentors.

I'll call the second reason the I-want-it-for-free mentality. I have studied some of the multi-millionaires in the world, such as Robert Kiyosaki and Grant Cardone; their mentorships, most times, are paid for. While industry leaders may offer some courses or seminars for free, most of the important content and information they are willing to share come with a price tag. This is understandable, as I have found out that what people do not pay for, they do not pay attention to.

The last reason which I have observed is laziness. Having been mentored and having mentored others myself, I've seen that mentorship pushes you and insists on certain uncomfortable but necessary adjustments.

You will be given books to read with very tight timelines to summarise and give action plans based on them. You may even be required to study and contribute to topics that you do not find interesting. In a nutshell, you will be pushed out of your comfort zone.

Naturally, we all prefer to remain in our comfort zones, but we must understand that real growth happens just outside the boundaries of that zone. None of the thought leaders I know got to where they are on a bed of comfort.

The Role of Personal Branding in Becoming an Authority

Remember the three types of people in the workplace today discussed in Chapter Three:

- Those who know but don't talk: These people leave you shocked at the results they produce. You find yourself making comments like, 'Oh my God, but she's so quiet!' or 'Oh, dear. I didn't know that he knew this'. They are the very smart people who, for their lack of ability to sell themselves and be vocal about what they do, mostly end up being overlooked.
- Those who know nothing but talk a good game: These are sometimes called the 'empty barrels'. They make so much noise that you think they know exactly what to do. Yet when you give them a task, they goof completely.
- Those who know what they are doing and can talk about it: This is the least populated set. These are the ones we aspire to be like because they are fully loaded barrels and make the loudest and most impactful noise.

There is no point in lighting a candle and putting it under your bed, especially if you are in a dark room. If you are talented at your work, you must be willing and ready to let people know this.

Let people know that you were invited to place X or place Y to speak, that you were invited to a panel to give a thought, or that you organised a webinar. Let people begin to see how much you are worth and how much you know.

I wish I had known this back then. I have no records of the first ten places I delivered a speech or talk because nobody told me to start building a profile, and I didn't have it in mind either. But a few years ago, I began to build my LinkedIn profile and update it with all my speaking engagements. And guess what. The more I updated my profile, the more people knew that I was speaking at events, the more the industry began to recognise that I was a good speaker, and the more speaking engagements I got.

As you grow in influence, you may need a PR team to manage your content, capture events, and help edit your articles. I must add that concerning personal branding, two other things are crucial.

- **You must have a strong LinkedIn profile as a career person**

This is important for you because LinkedIn is a new career market. It helps your visibility. In some countries, if you do not have endorsements on LinkedIn for some of the skills you claim to possess, you will never be contacted for them.

You should consider being trained on how to write a profile, optimise your LinkedIn page, and improve your visibility and job chances.

- **You must have profound content on the internet**

It amazes me how many people google their favourite religious, music, and sports celebrities but never search their own names to find out what internet footprints they have created.

In 2018 I did an assessment, searching for my name on Google. I was not satisfied with the search result, so I challenged myself to develop a roadmap that would, in four years, completely change my story. As you can tell, my story has indeed changed now.

The next time you google your favourite celebrity or an interesting story you heard online, also put your name on Google to find out how much content you have put out there and what perception you are selling about yourself.

When you pay more attention to your personal branding, you will see a marked difference in how people approach and engage you.

CHAPTER 8

PLANNING FOR RETIREMENT

It is quite uncommon for someone in their thirties to talk about retirement, especially in this part of the world. Yet, the subject of retirement is one aspect of a career that should be planned and prepared for with all intentionality.

Planning for retirement means being intentional about the plans you are putting in place to have a successful retirement.

From the conversations I have had with people about retirement, it seems most people begin to plan for retirement in their fifties or forties, while others leave it to chance. One of the things I have learned from mentors who have been able to retire into wealth – not into a pension – is that they started planning their retirement early. Wisdom told me I should also start planning my retirement early to achieve similar results.

I am sure you will have examples, as I do, of people who were Senior Managers, Directors, Chief HR Managers, Chief Financial Officers, and Chief Information Officers, who, after they lost their job or retired, struggled to maintain the same standard of living they had while working. Some of them cannot even afford the basics, such as school fees for their children, family vacation, or shopping. And this does not just happen to career people alone; it happens to everyone who does not plan for the 'dry' season during the 'rainy' season.

Whether you are into sports, entertainment, etc., or as a career person, it's important that you speak to your financial adviser to prepare a financial plan for your retirement.

While you try to accelerate your career quickly and get to the executive level, you should also start planning your retirement. You need to have other sources of income you can leverage. The questions to be asked here are: Have you started investing? If you lose your job today, what income would you be earning? What percentage of your salary do you save? Have you developed healthy financial habits that can sustain you regardless of change?

No one saw COVID-19 coming, but we all had to deal with it. You can build adaptability and resilience into your financial habits, allowing you to sail regardless of external changes.

These are some reasons why you need to start planning for retirement as early as your thirties:

Firstly, if you do not start early, you will regret it in the future. I learned this from my senior colleagues and some people in their fifties. If you are not disciplined with your finances in your thirties, you will end up paying for it.

Some put it this way: 'Play now, pay later, or pay now, play later'.

Secondly, you should always know that your bigger expenses are ahead of you. This means that the biggest bill you will ever pay is the bill you haven't paid yet.

You may think that your bills can't get any worse because you pay for rent, fees, clothing, feeding, and if you are from Africa, you probably send money to your family. However, that isn't the case, you may have to speak with people in their fifties and sixties about your current bills, and they will give you an idea of what more you have coming.

Just remember again that your biggest bills are ahead of you. If you do not start saving and having an investment plan now, you may run into trouble in the future.

However, if you start planning early for retirement, you probably have a lot of time to use your active income to create several streams of passive income.

Thirdly, you will have enough time to make mistakes and try again. I know a few people in their fifties who had kept all their savings and decided to start a business with them after they had retired. And in many cases, the business didn't do well, and all their life savings went down the drain.

It is difficult to start saving all over again at fifty-five or sixty. But if a business you invest in doesn't do well in your thirties, you can bounce back and retry since you still have about twenty more years of active work ahead of you.

The fourth and last reason is that financial freedom takes a while to attain.

Some people want to hit the jackpot and go from zero dollars today to a million dollars tomorrow. While this may be possible through some miracle, the miracle itself is not a financial strategy. When I teach, I show people how to plan so that their financial structure is stable and solid, and it's easier if they start in their thirties.

Since it takes a while to build financial structures to achieve financial independence, it is wiser to start early.

Building a Solid Wealth Model

Let me quickly point this out: The goal is financial independence and accelerating your career quickly to be able to earn a lot more than you would have earned if you remained on the same level for years. At this point, money begins to work for you, not you working for money.

I will mention three things you can do to build this sort of model:

- Start saving

Career people generally want to talk about their last vacation spot, where they order the newest phone online, the school their kids attend, and more. You may spend excessively on things you do not necessarily need, especially if they are unplanned expenses or impulsive buying. Paying for a bag and a shoe you do not need simply because of pressure from your colleagues is wrong.

Time passes by very fast. You will wake up one morning when you are forty-five or fifty and ask yourself what you did with all the money you earned in the past fifteen or twenty years.

Your savings habit has nothing to do with the amount you earn; it's all about the culture. If you don't save when you earn two hundred dollars, you'll have the same problem when you earn a million dollars. It is important to learn to avoid self-gratification and to create a healthy saving culture.

- Invest your savings

Invest in things with advice from your financial adviser. Do not go into investments without a proper financial adviser. There are stocks, bonds, real estate, start-ups, agriculture, and many other options that your financial adviser and mentor can help you with. Ensure that you begin to invest and earn some other income.

The major purpose of saving is no longer for a rainy day but for investment, such that the investment produces consistent income even without you working.

- Speak with a mentor

Several times, especially in our twenties and thirties, we come up with business ideas that we think are ground-breaking. However, most of those ideas have been tried by other people and probably didn't work out. Yet, we create assumptions about how those things work, especially when we look at businesses or investment opportunities from the outside.

What a mentor does for you in investing your savings is to guide you, especially in the area you have previously invested in. They tell you when the market is doing well, when to put in your money, and when the market will be potentially robust. They also tell you the areas to look out for and the mistakes they made so that you won't take a serious financial hit on all your savings.

Myths About Retirement

Many people hold some beliefs and assumptions about retirement only to find out later that they're false when it is too late. These are some myths about retirement that I have heard from older people:

- Myth 1: I will start saving later

This is a trap that many people in their thirties and early forties fall into. It always feels like, 'Let's enjoy the money we are making now; we'll talk about savings later'. But this only takes responsibility for your savings away from you and puts you in a place where you lack control. This is why some people go into depression when they lose their jobs.

Some who travel abroad say, 'I have migrated to the developed world, so the government will take care of me'. While I understand this, I know people who migrated to the developed world and found out that without savings, it's only a matter of time before you run into bankruptcy and serious credit problems.

- Myth 2: I will rely on my pension

In Nigeria, some government officials have been denied their pensions because of corruption around people's pensions and retirement benefits. Many eventually die trying to get them. There is no guarantee that you'd be able to live off your pension and retirement benefits, especially in this part of the world.

Also, remember that the value of a pension isn't what it used to be 10 to 15 years ago. Inflation has dealt a huge blow to it. What ten thousand dollars could afford ten years ago cannot be afforded by the same amount now.

You should know that every financial strategy that takes responsibility from you and puts it either on the government, infrastructure, your employer, or just on the force of nature is not sustainable and dependable.

- Myth 3: When I retire,
  I will open a consulting company

Most people close to retirement always feel they have much knowledge to share. They have gained a lot of experience in their company, so it makes sense to say, 'Once I retire, I will open a consulting company and help people out in the field that I gained experience in'.

While this is understandable and possible, I have seen it backfire for several people because it is based on too many assumptions. One of these assumptions is that companies will need their services. Another is that they have the right relationships in various organisations to convert their knowledge monetarily.

Running a consulting company is more than having the 'know-how' to put forward. There are costs around marketing, branding, staff cost, etc. There are also factors outside your control, such as the amount the companies will be willing to pay, and finally, there is competition too.

All these wrong assumptions and uncontrollable factors are the reasons it has not worked out for many people.

- Myth 4: My friends will support my business

This statement has also backfired for several people. For example, a friend of mine had friends that were executives like himself when he was about to retire in one of the biggest telecommunication industries. He had served at that executive level and sustained a career that had spanned thirty-eight to thirty-nine years. Truly, at that level, it is expected that his friends would support him when he tries to start a business in the telecommunication chain.

However, one of the mistakes he told me was assuming his friends would help him and they will be the first company on his profile. That way, he can use it to get new clients. This is a big assumption because anything could happen, and they could fail.

Two of these friends he banked on did fail. He believed that as soon as his proposal got to their table, it would be a closed deal, but COVID-19 happened, and the project never saw the light of day.

* * *

I may not be a financial adviser or a finance expert, but the truth is that you'll someday retire. Then you'll live with the decision you made while in active service.

My counsel is that you get a mentor and a financial adviser and begin a plan for your retirement. If you have passed your thirties and are reading this book, you may think that time has gone, but I believe the right time to start is the day that you get clarity about what you are supposed to do. Therefore, you need to start planning for your retirement today.

CONCLUSION

If you read this book from the beginning to this point, some of the many important things you may have noticed that I emphasised are the few ingredients required to build a strong foundation for an accelerated career. The emphasis speaks of their importance as there are no shortcuts.

The key element you need to have as an individual to successfully climb the corporate ladder to the pinnacle, even at a young age, has been expatiated in this book.

You've learned the importance of maintaining a good relationship with your line managers, receiving and implementing feedback, and then taking responsibility for your actions and their outcomes as you progress in your career path.

Another thing mentioned is that when you occupy a technical or professional role, you need to be a subject matter expert. By this, I don't mean that you are expected to know everything about your profession. However, you should be able to identify and understand where you are, the different interventions needed to become better at your career, and the training you may need to make that happen.

The fact remains – when it comes to career progression and acceleration, there are different stages. And for each stage you climb, there are various requirements: getting out fresh from college, becoming a specialist, mid-level manager, senior manager, and finally, an executive.

Also, from the perspective of this book, I have presented different angles on career progression.

The first is the preparatory stage, where you ask these questions: What goals are you setting? What values are core to you? What kind of competencies do you need?

If you do not have these properly set, it would be synonymous with trying to accelerate without gas in your car's tank, leaving you – the driver – frustrated. You will end up blaming the car and its internal components for not working when it is your responsibility to put gas in the car's tank for the engine to run.

After sorting out the preparatory phase, I discussed how to plan. Think of yourself as a chef looking to make a delicious meal called 'successful and accelerated career'. Firstly, you have to list the ingredients you need before going to the market to get them. Before stepping into the kitchen to cook, you must ensure the ingredients and food items available align with the meal you want to cook. And this explains why your career plan has to align with your career goals and objectives that you had set earlier.

Then, I discussed the execution phase, where you learned about the things to actively do while in employment, skills you need to have, relationships you need to build and some you need to let go of, and of course, how to play office politics. These are the things to ponder as you try to make your 'meal'.

Think about this phase as the time to get the measurements right, putting in the right amount of salt, water, seasonings, etc. These are the things that add up to produce what would be a successful career.

Finally, I spoke about planning for retirement and managing seasons of excess 'rain' so that when the 'dry' season comes, you do not suffer.

I truly hope that this book has inspired you, and if there is anything I want you to remember at the end, it is that your character will ultimately determine how far you go, regardless of all the tools and steps in this book.

Your success in career acceleration will always be limited to the character capacity you possess.

As feedback comes on various areas you could improve on – especially in your early career days – make due changes. For example, improve on report writing, improve the quality of your work, learn how to manage relationships, pay more attention to details, and have a personal development plan.

Make adjustments continuously, leaving nothing to chance or assumptions. Not being intentional about career growth will hinder you from achieving your full potential in your career and other areas of your life.

I hope to see everyone that reads this at the top, driving positive change and multiplying success stories.

AUTHOR'S PROFILE

Fene Osakwe is a multiple award-winning Global Tech professional, conference speaker, and Forbes-published author with over a decade of experience working in multibillion-dollar companies. He consults for several financial institutions, telecoms and fintech companies, state governments, and other Professionals, just as he sits on the advisory board of several companies across the globe.

Born in Southern Nigeria with very humble beginnings, Dr Fene is regarded as one of Africa's leading cybersecurity advisors and a highly sought-after career coach for career acceleration. He mentors hundreds of career professionals with a mission to help them rise from being fresh graduates to executive management in less than ten years, just like himself.

In 2021, Dr Fene was awarded an honorary Doctor of Business Administration (Leadership and innovation) from the Swiss School of Business Geneva and was invited into the exclusive Forbes Technology council in

2022, making him one of the few persons to make the Tech Council in their thirties.

He recently launched the Feneosakwe Foundation with a mission to empower the African child with the right tech skill to compete in today's world.

In this book, he chronicles his career journey, mistakes made, lessons learnt, principles applied, and how other career professionals can replicate his success in a much shorter time.

Made in the USA
Columbia, SC
17 July 2025

60859991R00089